For my mother for her example
and for my husband for his patience

Raffaella Serena

Embroideries & Patterns of Nineteenth Century Vienna

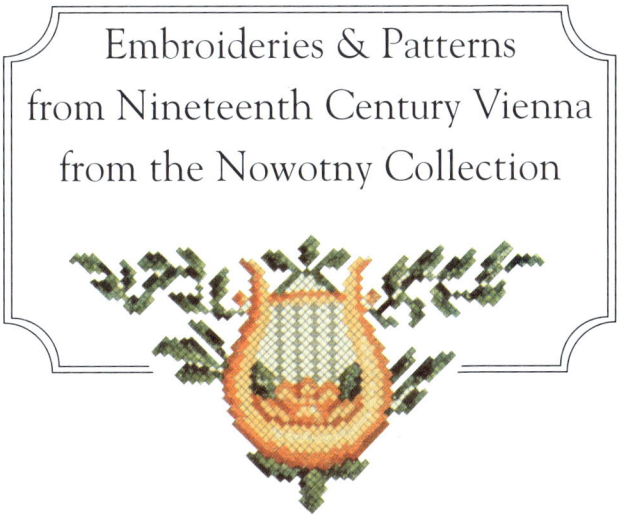

Embroideries & Patterns
from Nineteenth Century Vienna
from the Nowotny Collection

Antique Collectors' Club

Acknowledgemnts
The author and Idea books would like to thank Annelise and
Wolf Dieter von Primavesi for their invaluable assistance;
Renate Hiebner for her participation;
Chiara Uboldi for help with revisions;
and RenderLAB, Milan.

All embroidery patterns, if not otherwise acknowledged, are the
property of the Nowotny collection in Vienna.

Embroidery patterns from pages 166 to 206
are the work of Raffaella Serena.

Publishing co-ordination: Angela Passigli
Editorial: Fabiola Somaschini
Art Director: Pier Paolo Pitacco
Layout: Sonia Zavoli
Colour: F.G.V. & C., Milan
Printing: Stampa Nazionale, Florence

Copyright 1998
Idea Books Srl
via Cappuccio, 18
20123 Milan

This edition published 1998
Antique Collectors' Club,
5 Church Street, Woodbridge, Suffolk, UK.

ISBN 1 85149 283 6

All rights reserved. No part of this publication may be reproduced, stored in a retrieval system, or transmitted in any form or by any means, mechanical, photocopying or otherwise, without the prior permission of the publisher.

British Cataloguing-in-Publication Data
A catalogue record for this book is available from the British library

The right of Raffaela Serena to be identified as the author of this work has been asserted in accordance with the Copyright, Designs and Patents Act, 1988

Printed in Italy

Pullman Rd., Wigston, Leics. LE18 2DY, UK

Table of Contents

Introduction 7
Chapter 1 11
    The Nowotny Collection
Chapter 2 21
    Famous Names
Chapter 3 27
    Marie-Louise, Duchess of Parma
Chapter 4 37
    A Difficult Choice
Chapter 5 45
    The Biedermeier Period
Chapter 6 65
    Berlin Work
Chapter 7 79
    An Undervalued Art
    Bouquets and corners 90
    Garlands and butterflies 112
    Floral borders 126
    Details 140
    Upholstery 148
    Small Objects 152
    Embroidery and music 158
How to use the Patterns 164
Patterns 166
Bibliography 207

Introduction

Following the publication of my first book, *Stitch by Stitch*, I often considered bringing out a new book on needlework. In recent years there has been an increase in the number of people interested in this branch of the decorative arts, many of them seeking new sources of inspiration and fresh subject areas on which to practise.

The idea of writing about matters which will only interest needlework enthusiasts would be a very restrictive one but although most of the patterns and designs reproduced in this book were initially created for the practice of needlework, almost all of them can be applied to other artistic mediums as well. My hope is that this work will also be of interest to people with a general interest in the decorative arts.

The critical event that led to the writing of this book was my recent discovery of the Nowotny collection in Vienna, a collection that is unique both in the quantity and quality of its patterns and which is also a comprehensive historical record of some of the most refined and elegant creations of the nineteenth century. The breadth of the collection is such that there is an enormous selection from which to pick specific examples whilst at the same time it provides a source of lesser known and harder to find material. I have integrated the most significant patterns of the Nowotny collection with examples drawn from other sources in order to give a fuller and more complete historical and stylistic account of the period under

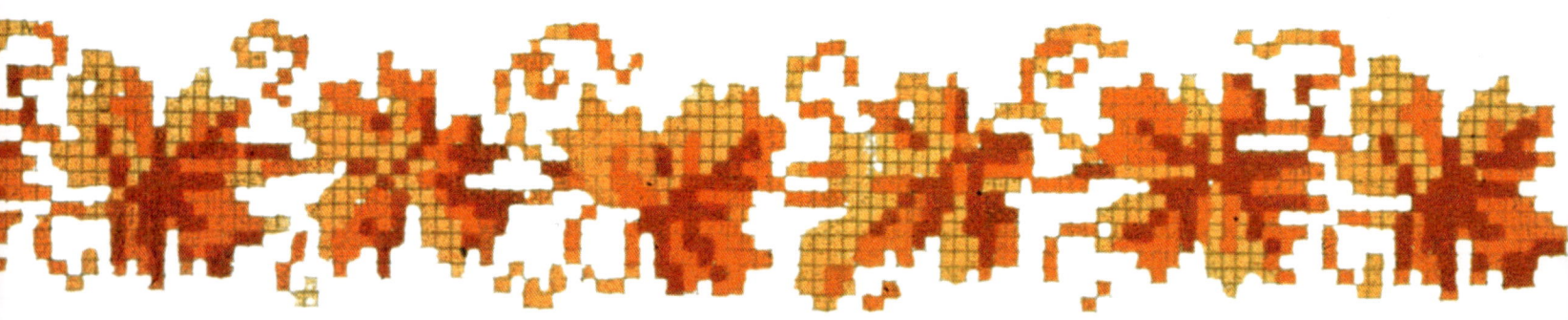

consideration, that of Biedermeier at the peak of its influence in the first half of the nineteenth century.

For many years now I have devoted myself to the research and study of decoration in all its aspects and in the widest sense of the word. I have always had an insatiable curiosity about a seemingly innate and universal human trait - the devotion of time, patience, and both intellectual and physical energy to embellishing anything and everything we create with flowers, animals, hieroglyphs, geometric figures and the like. My interest in the minor arts was passed on to me by my mother whom I used to accompany on her shopping expeditions which did not always culminate in purchases: her final choice was made solely on the basis of good taste, culture and personal sensitivity.

In my adolescent years I did not always share her enthusiasm. I confess that at times I would become bored in shops which only she - or so it seemed to me - could find interesting. I understood nonetheless that in addition to being endowed with an innate artistic sensibility, she had a feeling for the objects she loved which transcended aesthetic fulfilment; she respected and cared for those objects as if they were living creatures and spoke 'of the soul of things'... In her hands even simple bunches of flowers were transformed into wonderful arrangements of balanced and graceful elegance.

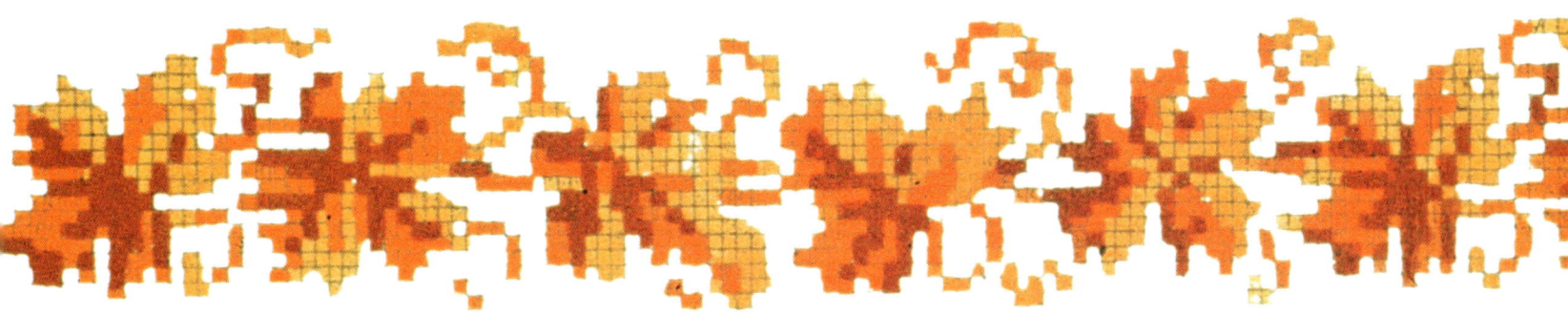

In later years I came to appreciate, share in and knowingly cherish the surroundings which in my childhood I had taken for granted. I then attempted to apply reason and order to what had always been for my mother an instinctive pleasure. My own interests turned to the applied and decorative arts which embrace all those objects and man made items which were created for practical usage and consequently were made with care and thought for their appearance and beauty as part of tradition and individual evolution.

My main source material came naturally enough from books and visits to museums and private collections. These reflect the personal agendas of the writer who describes or the collector who acquires such objects as have caught their fancy and have come to be part of their own private culture. The aim of a museum exhibit in historical and educational terms is to put together material for the future; through the objects on show the visitor comes in contact with practices, customs, taste and culture, all of which accurately reveal the evolution of history. Both books and museums are structured on the basis of well defined criteria or goals which at times may appear rather pedantic and seem to take away the spontaneity and excitement of the quest. I believe instead that it is just these structures which give a basis for a more rational evaluation: the museum, in denying us the ownership of the objects on display, gives a greater sense of detachment and 'unsullied' involvement.

However, I have recently had cause to see things quite differently.

4 Freisingergasse, Vienna, site of the original Nowotny enterprise in a XIVth century palace

The Nowotny Collection

CHAPTER 1

I visited Vienna in order to view for myself specific embroidery patterns. These came from a shop which had been trading for nearly two centuries, and I must admit that when I reached my destination I was in an unusually emotional state of anticipation. I already knew that the patterns that came from this venerable establishment were remarkable both in quantity and quality, but what I came upon was to surpass my fondest dreams. The panelled walls of the office and the workshop were lined with drawers and shelves filled to the brim with patterns - about five thousand of them - in a variety of styles which included work by major nineteenth century artists. The subject matter ran the full gamut from animals and flowers to landscapes and borders and included upholstery patterns. All were exquisite.

The firm was established in 1818 by a Moravian immigrant, Anton Nowotny, who together with his Viennese wife, Josefin Durr, ran the business up until the time of his death. Located in the heart of old Vienna, the shop carried a stock of items that could satisfy every possible embroidery need: wool and silk thread, chenille, beads, étamines, linen, canvas, and patterns, they were all there. In 1855 Ludwig Nowotny took over the business from his father and applied himself to it with such

Opposite. An important embroidery chart depicting a parrot resting on a magnificent basket of flowers.

energy that the shop gained world renown, as can be seen by leafing through the old ledgers which recorded the names of his customers. From Brussels the firm imported superior quality linen thread for lace making at a time when top-grade linen was worth its weight in gold many times over: a half-kilo cost 1200 gulden, a fortune in those days. In 1890 Ludwig Nowotny II took over the reins in turn; he is best remembered for the numerous Romanian, Hungarian and Czechoslovakian folk patterns collected in the course of his travels throughout the

Opposite. An elegant border with friezes and flowers.

Above. An embroidery chart by Muller showing a luxuriant garden with figures.

dominions of the Hapsburg monarchy. The last descendant Desirée Richter, the daughter of Ludwig Nowotny II, carried on the family business to a ripe old age. She passed away in 1996 at the age of ninety.

In 1993 the shop was taken over by Annelise von Primavesi, a delightful Austrian lady with a professional background in chemical engineering.

Amongst her personal reasons for this unusual career change, must have been her passion for the arts, her interest in antiques and her determination to preserve intact a veritable treasure trove of patterns which I suspect is unique.

Over the years merchandise sold by the Nowotny firm has been unsurpassed for its style, artistry and value. Each of the various proprietors made a practice of commissioning leading designers of the day, amongst whom were three painters of the Viennese School, to create original patterns of exceptional refinement. In addition to making use of the design plates issued by various contemporary publishing houses, the firm availed itself of works produced by artists known as 'stitch painters' who had the knack

Opposite. A splendid bouquet with white lilies and pink roses.

Top and below right. A casket for embroidery materials in mother-of-pearl and gilded bronze. Vienna, 1825-1830. Courtesy Philippe Gentil. Above. Embroidery casket. Germany, 1835.

16

Above. A chart by E. Muller with various motifs typical of the Biedermeier period. Courtesy Wurttembergisches Landesmuseum, Stuttgart.

(embroidery pattern p.188, 204)

of using paintings as inspiration for embroidery patterns. The firm not only dealt in embroidery materials but was also involved in the creation and manufacture of precious objects such as nécessaires and in the design of furnishings whose predominant motif was embroidery. The shop which belonged to the same family for so long still keeps the name of its most illustrious owner, Ludwig Nowotny. It remains housed at its original location in a fourteenth century building at 4 Freisingergasse in the heart of Vienna just a short distance from St Stephen's.

Opposite. A chart with unusual shading.

Monogram of an aristocrat from the Hapsburg era.

Famous Names

CHAPTER 2

Amongst the many unrecorded anecdotes and reminiscences about old Viennese society are those which record the remarkably close relations which existed between the Court and the shopkeepers. It was an era when archduchesses and ladies of both the aristocracy and the bourgeoisie alike took delight in embroidery. In the records of the Nowotny business the names of well-known customers frequently occur.

The most illustrious was that of Elizabeth, Empress of Austria, better known as Sissy. One particular story about her has been handed down over the years - I heard it myself from Annelise von Primavesi. As the story goes the Nowotny family was roused in the middle of the night by a court emissary with a request to open up the shop and supply some embroidery for the capricious and impulsive Sissy.

For the wedding of the Archduchess Valerie (Sissy's daughter) with the Archduke Franz Salvator of Tuscany, the Empress commissioned a needlework nécessaire. The Nowotny firm made an iron trunk for the young bride. Its exterior was not particularly handsome but inside it had velvet lined partitions with room for everything that an embroidery enthusiast might need: a vast assortment of thread, silk of every hue, ribbons of every sort, needles,

Opposite. A chart with floral motif featuring reds and blues with a green and gilded bronze vase.

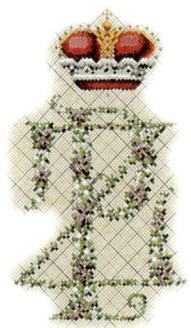

Above. A monogram of an aristocrat of the Hapsburg era composed of many small flowers.

Below. An artistic composition with a quantity of flowers arranged in an elegant colour scheme.

scissors and the finest linens. Other prominent customers included Sissy's sisters Marie of Bavaria, wife of Francesco II, King of the Two Sicilies and Mathilda, Countess of Trani and wife of Ludovico di Bourbon, brother of Francesco II. Countess Chotek, a lady-in-waiting to the Empress Sissy, was likewise an assiduous customer of the Freissingergasse shop. It was she who married Crown Prince Franz Ferdinand only to be subsequently assassinated with him at Sarajevo.

Amongst the ladies of the aristocracy and the court we must not overlook the Archduchess Sophie, Franz Josef's mother, who in addition to being an accomplished embroideress in her own right,

Above. A design representing a white dove spreading its wings amid roses, lilies and lilac.

also took it upon herself to promote the craft. Leafing through orders taken at the end of the nineteenth century we come across the names of loyal Nowotny customers who were well known in the fields of literature, medicine, music and industry. Amongst them were the following: the Baroness Berta von Sutter, Austrian pacifist and writer, who was awarded the Nobel Prize in 1905; the noble Hungarian Esterhazy family which had once been the patron of Haydn and whose holdings in 1870 included twenty-one castles, four hundred and fourteen villages and sixty towns; the family of the celebrated physician Professor Billroth, founder of the celebrated Viennese school of medicine; and the Richard Strauss family whose descendants still patronise the shop. So numerous are the famous names connected with Nowotny that a review of all them would be a veritable chronicle of a century of European history.

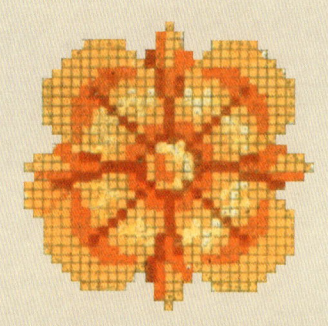

G. Naudin, Parma. A drawing room, 1832

Marie Louise
Duchess of Parma

CHAPTER 3

We shall speak at length of Marie-Louise, not only because her role in history is well known, but also because we can get very close to her as we learn about her feelings, her tastes, her personality, and her likes and dislikes thanks to the rich collection of letters, memories and objects she left for posterity. Indeed we can get to know her as a woman. Certain folders containing original embroidery patterns, many naturally originating from Vienna, are preserved in Parma's Glauco Lombardi Museum which is dedicated to the Duchess. There are water-colours by Marie-Louise herself, painted on squared paper, and there are also some of the pattern notes in her own handwriting which give a running commentary on the composition, the colour schemes and the work projects

Opposite. A canvas designed and embroidered by Marie-Louise. Courtesy Museo G. Lombardi, Parma.

Below. Floral border with roses and campanulas

Above. A pair of splendid floral motifs by Müller.

with their variegated yarns. The flowers which Marie-Louise was so fond of form the subject matter of the collection: '...the writing paper is headed with flowers and flowers of every sort are scattered everywhere: flowers from the garden, in vases, painted in water-colours, embroidered in silk, cut from velvet, composed from sea-shells ...'[1]. The extent of the sovereign's interest in the craft is obvious from the caskets, the embroidery nécessaires and the number of boxes filled with spools, silk thread of every colour, chenille, ribbons and unfinished embroidery projects. The Duchess was especially fond of upholstery and cross stitch on canvas. She had learned the art as a child in Vienna where she often gave her small creations as presents to family members as well as to her governess, Countess Colloredo.

Even when she became Empress of France embroidery remained one of her favourite occupations. Her hobby did not escape Napoleon's notice since he conscientiously insisted on obtaining information about the tastes and personality of his betrothed with whom he was not acquainted but whom he was to wed by proxy. It is worth relating an incident which epitomises what is meant by a 'sensitive man'. On March 13, 1810 the marriage by proxy of the eighteen-year-old Archduchess Marie-Louise of Hapsburg

and the Emperor of the French was celebrated. Escorted by an imposing retinue the bride set off for Paris. Three days later the bridal procession reached Braunau-on-Inn where, in accordance with the prearranged ceremony, the Archduchess was 'consigned' to France. The party continued on its way towards Compiègne where Marie-Louise was to meet the Emperor.

Above.
A rose and lilac floral border.

We can imagine her state of mind: the grief in her heart, the sense of abandonment and the need to hide her feelings as she travelled amongst strangers towards the impending meeting with the man whom ever since childhood she had been taught to hate as the enemy of Austria, and who was now her husband. The encounter between the newlyweds had been planned down to the

finest detail and the precise ceremony left nothing to chance: the introduction to the French court of the new Empress, her genuflection before Napoleon as a sign of homage, each gesture, each word spoken by the protagonists and the formal code of dress. But, to the consternation of all, the Emperor broke with protocol and approached his bride unaccompanied: '...he was wearing the plain grey greatcoat that he had worn in so many battles ...'.[2] On horseback, soaked by the rain, impatient and wilful he halted the carriage of his bride and, as he later recalled, "...I dashed into the carriage and kissed Marie ..."[3]. It was not so much in the role of Emperor that he paid tribute to her with this display of impatient

Opposite left. A floral border with luxuriantly curling leaves and small roses. Opposite right. A floral border with roses and small blue flowers.

Below. A rich border of pink roses and white anemones intertwined with a blue ribbon.

(embroidery pattern p.192)

longing as in that of an ordinary man who wished to meet his wife free from the formal conventions imposed by their rank. Napoleon had the carriage continue on in the direction of Compiègne which the party reached late in the evening. There in her apartments Marie-Louise found a sumptuous corbeille as a gift from the Emperor. But her joy was unbounded when among the many presents she found her puppy, her songbirds and the unfinished embroidery that she had left behind in Vienna! In great secrecy Napoleon had seen to it that these things were brought to Compiègne, thus demonstrating an unusual degree of savoir-faire and sensitivity.

[1] Mario Praz *La filosofia dell'arredamento* (Milan: Longanesi, 1964).
[2] Irmgard Schiel, *Maria Luigia* (Milan: Longanesi, 1983).
[3] *Ibid.*

Marie-Louise's favourite bouquet: Parma violets (embroidery pattern p.172)
Opposite. A classical motif showing small temple and urn in a garden setting. Courtesy Textilmuseum, St Gallen.

A female figure plaiting a garland of roses in a garden in full bloom. Courtesy Nowotny Collection

A difficult choice

CHAPTER 4

A chart with various motifs: a landscape, two butterflies and a border with typical designs of the period.

But now let us return to Vienna and the famous shop on Freisingergasse. During my stay in the city I spent days on end viewing and evaluating a wealth of patterns nearly all of which were of considerable interest.

Their attraction is enhanced by the wear and tear they have undergone over the years. They served first as shop samples for customers, after which they were given to female workers who prepared the canvas on which the pattern was outlined, and then were finally passed on to the purchaser, complete with yarn ready for embroidering.

Even today kits from Nowotny are made up in the same traditional way: the pattern is not printed on the canvas, nor is there a chart laid out on squared paper. Instead the patterns are outlined on the canvas with coloured threads arranged in lines. All the embroideress has to do is to embroider her petit point using the threads as a guide. Many such patterns were personally completed by the customer while certain wealthy clients preferred to leave the task to Nowotny. This was also the case with large or complex works. It was naturally possible to purchase the pattern on its own, in which case the embroideress herself would choose the type of étamine on which to embroider, the sort of yarn

A chart embroidered with a garland motif of oak leaves and acorns. Below. The same motif on canvas.

Corners with floral motifs by Müller - above pink campanulas, below oak leaves and acorns.

Opposite. Three borders with different subjects by Paterno.

to use - either in silk or wool - and she would decide whether or not to make use of beads.

The choices made depended on the purpose for which the work was destined, be it a cushion, a fire screen, a handbag or an album cover. Upholstery work was always done in petit point with wool because of its greater resistance to wear and tear. This would be the case with sofas, armchairs and other chairs, footstools and rugs. For aesthetic reasons silk thread was used for the lighter-coloured parts to obtain a chiaroscuro effect which gave the work a greater sense of depth.

If the work called for the inclusion of figures these were embroidered in particularly fine stitching with a single thread which made the figures stand out from their backgrounds. Such work also required a bigger range of colours for detailed work on faces and hands.

Other objects such as fire screens, tea cosies, album covers, handbags and cushions could be done in petit point or cross stitch using wool, silk, chenille or beads. Sometimes only a single type of yarn was used but more often there were many and this had the advantage of conferring a richer, more variegated appearance to the work. For handbags beads were used almost exclusively. Beads were further utilised in more fanciful works such as covers for drinking glasses, cigar and other boxes, and picture frames. In some countries beads were frequently pre-selected to match the yarn in order to produce a

Above. A chart by Müller with various small motifs to be used according to the taste or needs of the embroideress.

wide variety of subject matter which had traditionally been embroidered in wool or silk.

All these different kinds of work were based on the patterns on squared paper put out by the various publishing houses of the day. The choice of subject like the choice of material was exclusively determined by the imagination, taste and aesthetic sensibility of the embroideress. As can be seen from the illustrations reproduced in this book, it was often the case that a variety of motifs was grouped together, each of which might be used on its own as a decorative element in other works. In this case the choice of colour, too, was left to the embroideress since in the early years the colours were not specified with the pattern. As my researches have frequently borne out, embroideries based on the same pattern often show differing colour tones.

It proved truly difficult for me to decide on the theme of this book since almost all the examples I came across, some five thousand in number, were worthy of inclusion. Overwhelmed by the work in prospect due to the mass of heterogeneous, totally unclassified material I was faced with, I decided to let things settle of their own accord and devote myself to other matters for a while. And so I went about the city in search of distraction. I browsed in bookstores, lingered in antique shops and visited certain museums as well as a delightful Biedermeier house. The fortunate outcome of my museum visits was that I re-acquired the necessary lucidity to enable me to return to my systematic examination and thus I successfully completed a task that initially had appeared difficult indeed.

Below. A multi-coloured butterfly in the middle of a heart-shaped garland of leaves.

A typical Biedermeier interior using the same ornamental motifs which were used both for wall decoration and upholstery embroidered in petit point. Berlin Stadtmuseum, Berlin

The Biedermeier Period

CHAPTER 5

A table with typical lyre motif.

*Opposite.
A design with typical motifs of the Biedermeier period: swan, lyre, flowers.*

*I*n the course of my museum visits I looked at china, engraved and painted glass, furniture, jewelry, paintings, watches and albums of drawings for interior decoration or for china. I noticed that, in addition to common stylistic traits, the motifs were often used at random to decorate one object or another. Many of the subjects were identical to the ones I had just seen in the embroidery guides at the Nowotny shop. It was not that I was ignorant of the fact that in Vienna there had once been a flourishing embroidery pattern trade but rather that, having seen only a certain number of them, I had not yet come to fully appreciate the fact that this output was an integral part of a movement in which the applied arts developed widely during the Biedermeier period from 1815-1848.

As a matter of fact, when I returned to take a closer look at the huge collection at Nowotny's, I noticed that the patterns produced by the various publishing houses of the period were also in the same style. At this point all doubt vanished: my chosen task would not be to describe an important collection and to speak in general terms of a certain type of embroidery

A chart by Bermann with recurrent lyre motif framing a basket of flowers.

Below. A piece of furniture with the same motifs shown in the preceding embroidery plate. Courtesy Mondadori.

but rather to select the most representative subjects of the decorative taste of the period. The subject matter may seem commonplace, even banal, but as we shall see when it comes to Biedermeier there could be no other.

"The term Biedermeier is used in a narrow sense to designate a style of home furnishing and in a broad sense the culture of an entire historical period".[4] The period runs from the time of the end of the Napoleonic Wars and concludes with the Congress of Vienna, from 1815 to the 1848 uprisings. After the Congress of Vienna Francis I (1792-1835) established an absolutely inflexible, conservative regime in which common citizens were banned from participating in political affairs. Metternich was the architect of this strategy; in the police state he created, censorship reigned and any form of innovation, even cultural, was met with opposition. In such a climate the

A garland of laurel leaves framing a lyre.

Below. A small piece of furniture in the shape of a column with motifs similar to the preceding design.

Austrians, and particularly the Viennese, sought comfort in the simple pleasures of family life, in the love of nature and in music. Court life was marked by the same plainness of style and the years following a period of war and deprivation were characterised by a constant search for calm, for security and for the peace that everyone desired.

The home became the hub for social gatherings and literary and musical circles where everyone could express themselves in activities such as painting, embroidery and literature. The water-colours and paintings of interiors that were so fashionable in the nineteenth century still hold great interest today. They allow us to enter a meticulously detailed world where we become acquainted not only with a decorative fashion but above all with an approach and attitude to life. In the Biedermeier period the home would seem to have been designed

50

Opposite above. A china cup and plate with splendid floral and gold decoration. Courtesy Prestel. Opposite below. An identical rose border to that painted on cup provides the subject for this embroidery plate. Property of author. (embroidery pattern p.190)

to keep the outer world at bay: it was the expression of a culture based on the family environment in which daily life is made as pleasant as possible. The dominant theme in these interiors may be summed up in a sense of security, order, beauty and loving care for each individual object. The most important room in the house was the drawing room, no longer intended as the place to conduct formal affairs but rather as a meeting place for family and friends.

Above. An intricate grapevine pattern decorates and elegant Meissen coffee service. Courtesy Prestel.

An embroidery design by Müller with the same motif of leaves. Courtesy Stickmuster Museum, Celle.

Above. Three more vine-shoots by Müller. Property of author.

Furniture had also changed from the days of the Empire style with its overwhelming emphasis on decoration, massive size and a surfeit of ornamentation; Biedermeier furniture was designed for functionalism, comfort, elegance and restraint. The wood employed, briar, mahogany, cherry and pear, was selected with care for it was considered a fundamental decorative element in itself. Ornamentation was reduced to a minimum: symmetrical and neo-classical in taste, it was almost

The china plate and the embroidery chart on this page have a bouquet of pansies as their theme.

(embroidery pattern p.186)

A small basket of flowers embossed on the cover of a silver box. The composition recalls the embroidery chart above with roses and violets. Property of author.

Floral decoration painted on a glass in the same style as the design above.

(embroidery pattern p.201)

(embroidery pattern p.171)

An elegant glass engraved with the word 'souvenir'. Each letter is formed by tiny flowers. c.1820. Bayerisches Nationalmuseum, Munich.

Below. The letters in this alphabet are also composed of leaves and flowers in the same style as the glass. Courtesy Biblioteca Bertarelli, Milan.

invariably executed in ebony. The lyre is among the most typical decorative motifs: we find it as a support for tables, on the backs of chairs, as ebony inlay on columns and furniture, and painted on china cups and in needlework. In the delightful contemporary paintings of interiors one notes the extensive presence of glass cabinets and etagères which were designed to display small collections of china and glass objects.

The 'collectors' cups' produced by the celebrated Vienna China Works were among the most prized. Both engraved and painted drinking glasses were popular with their typical cylindrical shape, flared at the bottom. Often enough these objects were decorated with floral patterns or landscapes,

Above. Two elegant personal firescreens in silk painted with floral motifs. Private collection.

Above. A luxuriant floral motif painted on porcelain by Josef Nigg. Made in Vienna in 1840. Courtesy MAK-Österreichisches Museum für angewandte kunst, Vienna.

designs we also find in embroidery. In these interiors a secrétaire is invariably to be seen often surmounted by a clock in the form of a miniature temple. This temple theme was well represented in landscape paintings with their numerous urns intended for the burning of incense and flowers as a symbolic sacrifice to Cupid.

The love of nature was dominant and found expression in paintings and in homes where plants and flowers were ever present, whether fresh, dried, painted, inlaid on furniture,

Opposite. The same profusion of flowers is the theme of this marvellously complex embroidery plate.

Three delightful valentines with recurrent Biedermeier motifs. Courtesy Museo Etnografico di Dietenheim, Teodone, Brunico.

An embroidery chart with small designs similar in subject to the valentine cards opposite (embroideries patterns p.202, 205)

embroidered on sofas and easy-chairs or as part of wall friezes. This intimate environment consecrated to the joys of domestic life and brimming with poetry, harmony and elegance, and cut off from the outside world nonetheless did not exclude nature's presence; on the contrary nature was shown to its best advantage in the home. While people are only rarely depicted in these water-colours, there is a feminine presence in the needlework decorations: the fire screen, bell-pulls, easy-chairs

Above. A similar design on an embroidery chart with two doves amid flowers.
(embroideries patterns p.205, 206)

executed in petit point, footrests, albums frequently embroidered with beads, leather cigar-cases decorated with the finest chenille or silks, pretty little cards slipped into large mirrors, personal fire screens either embroidered or painted on silk and the inevitable small tables on which to rest one's work-basket. The words of Mario Praz in *The Philosophy of Interior Decoration* effectively express the emotion evoked by these miniature masterpieces of interiors which introduce us to a bygone world with all its charm: '... rooms light, fresh and simply adorned with stucco-work and medallions which serve as the background for the sharply defined forms of the mahogany furniture, the silver furnishings and the pieces of crystal mark a phase of human civilisation which is perhaps unsurpassed and where reserve was not dissociated from friendliness, practicality from elegance, reality from the world of dreams...a precious record of the interior design of the time.'

4 William M. Johnston *Vienna, Vienna* (Milan: Mondadori, 1981.

Below. A design printed in Vienna showing a small temple, a recurrent theme during the first half of the XIXth century.

A rose, a much loved flower in the Biedermeier period.
Stickmuster Museum, Celle (embroidery pattern p.189)

Berlin work

CHAPTER 6

Above. Two designs for corners with a profusion of curling leaves and flowers. Whilst slightly differing, they retain the same style.

Opposite. An elegant design showing a lyre entwined with a rose shoot and a branch of white flowers. Courtesy Wurttembergisches Landesmuseum, Stuttgart.

𝓘n 1986 I visited an important exhibition in Vienna on the Biedermeier period which, with the exception of embroidery, featured all sorts of manufactured items of the day. The same was true of the Biedermeier show held in Paris in 1990 at Bagatelle where embroidery was represented only by some exquisitely crafted needlework boxes. It is amazing how this particular area of the applied arts was completely ignored both in terms of finished items and patterns.

In the past this was an art reserved for professionals, whose

Berlin Verlag von G. Eduard Müller.

Previous pages. A chart by Sajou of Paris showing a camellia and a peony by the gooseberry bush. A basket overflowing with a profusion of flowers. Property of author.

Above. A Grecian temple in a garden.

customers came from the highest social classes, whose designers were famous artists and whose artisans were members of a school or professional association; with the nineteenth century the art became popular and available to everyone. The reason for the outstanding success and notable popularity enjoyed by petit point during the entire course of that century can be traced back to a simple but effective concept. In 1804 the Berlin publisher Phillison came out with the first pattern on squared paper where each square corresponded to a stitch. The patterns were first drawn by hand and then transferred to copper plates for printing keeping the division into squares clearly visible. Subsequently some were hand coloured with water-colours.

Each square corresponded with either a stitch, petit point, half stitch or cross stitch to be transferred to fabric with a regular weave, whether linen or canvas. This made it possible for anyone to complete complex projects; anyone, provided they had the patience, could purchase a pattern on squared paper and do an embroidery. The simplified technique thus contributed to the popular success of this type of work which could be completed as much by professional embroideresses as by private individuals at home.

Many publishers followed Philipson's example and so 'Berlin embroidery' or 'Berlin work' as it was known, achieved vast popularity in Europe and later on in the rest of the world, overshadowing every other type of needlework. The primary

Below pages. A garland of pansies, Italy. Property of author.

Above. A delightful design with a rural theme by Paterno.

(embroidery pattern p.194)

production centres were Berlin, Hamburg and Nuremberg where numerous publishing houses both large and small had offices. Specialist shops catering to embroidery needs sprang up all over Europe; Germany was the first to export hand-coloured patterns and later on albums printed on an industrial scale which achieved unprecedented popularity.

In Berlin B. Sommerfeld was the most important exporter for the publishing houses. This firm built up a world-wide business through shows and exhibitions such as the Great Exhibition at the Crystal Palace in London in 1851, as well as in America, China and Japan. Patterns were specially created for individual countries as can be seen from illustrations with oriental or religious subjects which were clearly destined for Russia and Greece. [5]

With thirty years in the business, L. W. Wittich was one of the more prominent German publishers. It was Wittich who came out with hand-coloured illustrations which were later published and sold individually, a formula that proved highly successful. He was also the first to export his designs to London, specifically to Wilks in Regent Street, which became the most famous shop in its line.

Beginning in 1830 Wilks improved its selection by the direct purchase of the best the international market had to offer, achieving unparalleled fame and fortune. The Wilks name and address were printed along with that of the publisher on every pattern and by 1840 the number of illustrations it had made available exceeded 14,000.

In France there was also a sizeable output of embroidery patterns. About 1820 Augustin Legrand was the first to publish an album of designs. Entitled *L'art de broder*, it contained twenty or so hand coloured patterns. From 1830 onwards production increased as various publishing houses were founded and

Below. A representation of a scissor shaped candle-snuffer, this design was probably intended for making a small bag. By Paterno.

Above. A festive garland with a variety of flowers and butterfly by Bermann. Some small sketches by the embroideress are clearly visible in background.

achieved fame either by launching specialist magazines themselves or else by illustrating the specialist magazines of others. These magazines achieved world fame. In 1834 the publisher Mallez founded the magazine *La brodeuse* whose needlepoint patterns were created by the publishing house of Sejou. Martin and Robert were other important publishers. Their output was prodigious as each of these houses published no less than thousands of designs, with the pattern number 9616 from Sejou appearing in *La brodeuse* [6].

In Austria Muller was the most famous publisher: in forty years of business activity he made available more than three thousand patterns. Of German origin, Muller began operating in the first

Opposite. A splendid bouquet of flowers.

decade of the nineteenth century in Vienna where he acquired the publishing house, Kunsthandler, to whose name he added the name of the street where their offices were located, Kohlmarkt, as can be seen on every illustration he ever published. Other publishers with a flourishing output included Paterno and Bermann.

In my view the Viennese patterns differ from the German ones. I find that the former show a lighter touch in the composition of patterns for both smaller and more complex works. My observations led to the conclusion that the Viennese had the more personal of the two styles. Perhaps the reason for this lies in the fact that Vienna lacked an international market as vast as the German one and that as a result the patterns were bound up to a greater extent with the taste of the place in which they were created.

[5] Josephine Laandwehr-Vogels, 'Historische kruissteekpatronen', Zomer & Keuning Boeken B.V., Ede, 1984.
[6] *ibidem*

*Below.
A delightful little garland of hydrangeas by Wittich. Courtesy Stickmuster Museum, Celle.*

(embroidery pattern p.197)

*A cornucopia with a charming bouquet of flowers.
Private collection*

An Undervalued Art

CHAPTER 7

A magnificent example of embroidery on linen taken from a Viennese design. Private collection.

As we have seen, there was a prodigious output of embroidery patterns in the nineteenth century which had an unprecedented success all over the world. Yet although under the heading 'Embroidery' in the various encyclopaedias there are exhaustive accounts of its origins, its history and the evolution of its various offshoots over the years, there is scarcely a mention of petit point in the last century The phenomenon universally known as 'Berlin work' is not considered worthy of attention, even as popular history. Nonetheless the experts responsible for writing the articles for the encyclopaedias could scarcely have been ignorant of the fame enjoyed by Berlin work, especially as there are museums and libraries that have devoted considerable attention to this genre, not just as a sociological aspect of female education in historical terms but also for its value as true art.

There have been times when I have had to forcefully insist with the textile curator in some museum or library in order to be allowed to view nineteenth century patterns or manufactured articles. In my opinion their presence in museum archives has been ignored because they were simply considered to be of little interest. Perhaps the fact that they were only the products of domesticity and made no pretence to historical importance or evidence of the taste of an era, has made it easy to brand these works as mere 'hobbies', unworthy of attention since their sole purpose was to decorate the home for the exclusive pleasure of the embroideress and her family.

Certainly the patterns that were printed and used in the nineteenth century were not, in terms of composition and

Below. Gracefully entwined flowers amongst which is a splendid clematis.

Above. A design with doves and flowers, a recurrent Biedermeier theme. Courtesy Wurttembergisches Landesmuseum, Stuttgart.

subject matter, comparable to masterpieces of the past such as the tapestries designed by great artists or produced by important schools or guilds. Up until the close of the eighteenth century the creation and making of embroidery belonged almost exclusively to the male world. I say this because where operative techniques were not terribly demanding the professional embroiderers were often aided by female workers employed outside the workshops.

Once Philipson's idea had made the petit point technique easily accessible to all, patterns became simpler in composition and were reduced in size. Publishers availed themselves of the work of good painters and designers for the creation of new

Three white doves on flower shoots on a blue and gilt bronze vase.

models; they were not the equal of the great names of the past but are still worthy of attention if we look on them as examples of the continuing evolution of one area of the decorative arts.

I thus find it curious that, in so many general books on the applied or the minor arts, authors who are sensitive and attentive to artistic merits in other areas never, and I use the word 'never' advisedly, mention nineteenth century embroidery or needlepoint tapestry. The subject is only ever covered by specialists in books concentrating on specific works or masterpieces.

I am not the only one to be amazed. In his book, *The Sense of Order. A Study on the Psychology of the Decorative Arts*, the

Viennese author Ernst Gombrich, probably the best known scholar in the field, tells us how he came to appreciate the attraction of decoration through the Slovakian peasant embroidery that his mother collected, and then continues: 'I well remember asking myself why such works were not considered 'art' on the same level as great paintings.'

I do not believe that the scholars in the field who fail to

Above. A white calla lily amongst roses and nasturtiums.

Opposite. A rich floral pattern for an armchair.

mention this genre do so out of insufficient knowledge since they write copiously on a wide variety of topics. I have a strong suspicion, bordering on certainty, that they deliberately avoid discussing it due to their preconceived notion that, if this type of work is not performed in a professional setting, it must necessarily be consigned to the world of 'little women' who amuse themselves with pointless pastimes. This conviction seems senseless to me if for no other reason than that the work of embroidering the upholstery for a sofa is extremely demanding, and the fact that this is done with a sense of

Above. A bunch of strawberries in a bouquet is the theme of this chart by Paterno.

pleasure and without remuneration in no way diminishes its substance or value

The true artist is the one who creates the pattern while the person who embroiders uses it to execute a work which at first sight has no other merit than that of a good level of patience. However, one should not forget that the choice of pattern is dependent on it fitting appropriately into an existing decorative setting. It must match its surroundings. At times it may even become the most important decorative element. Thus the choice of subject and its intended purpose involve aesthetic considerations. These also affect any modifications to the composition that the embroideress may choose to make, any personal choice of background colour and any of the finishing touches which make a given work unique even when seen against other reproductions of the same subject. It is like performing a piece of music: only rarely is the player also the composer; the music is usually written by others while it is the musician who interprets it and enjoys it. In her autobiography Agatha Christie relates that she started writing as a substitute for embroidery: 'I had formed a habit or writing stories by this time. It took the place, shall we say, of embroidering cushion covers ... If anyone thinks this is putting creative writing too low on the scale, I cannot agree. The creative urge can come out in any form.....I would agree that the embroidering of Victorian cushion covers is not equal to participating in the Bayeux Tapestry, but the urge is the same in both cases...the artist's inner satisfaction was probably much the same.'

The fact remains that those who write about the applied arts have little respect for the 'pastime' of embroidery: they tend to ignore all those nineteenth century designers who created the

Below. A small bunch of pansies by Muller.

(embroidery pattern p.178)

Above. Violets and roses are the theme of this splendid basket. Courtesy Textilmuseum, St Gallen.

Opposite. A rug with a magnificent composition of flowers in vivid colours.

many thousands of embroidery patterns which have a high aesthetic value.

The Nowotny collection forms an important part of this book because of the sheer quantity of plates and patterns in the collection which are unmatched by any museum. The quality of a great many of the subjects is outstanding and is attributable both to the favourable climate of the time when the Nowotny family were in business and to the refined tastes and wealth of the customers. This in turn attracted artists and designers with superb stylistic talents.

Bouquets and corners

Two splendid original floral compositions. Private collection (embroidery pattern p.174)

A bouquet of light blue hydrangias and white flowers (embroidery pattern p.182)

The same bouquet on canvas using different colours.

Opposite. A bunch of flowers and leaves with vivid colours.

Two bouquets of unusual flowers.

Above. A small bunch of light blue campanulas. Property of author (embroidery pattern p.173)

Opposite. White gardenias streaked with red form the subject of this Italian plate. Property of author.

Detail of a pattern (embroidery pattern p.170)

A simple but pleasing bouquet arrangement.

Two stylised roses and buds.
Courtesy Stickmuster Museum, Celle.

Detail of a floral motif with roses. Property of author.

A particularly beautiful spray of roses.

A small basket with flowers in quintessential Biedermeier style.

Two plates depicting rosebuds. (embroidery pattern p.203)

Above. A cheerful arrangement of poppies and cornflowers. Below. Simple but graceful small campanulas by Müller.

*Preceding pages. An important design for a cushion or small rug in bright delicate colours.
Above. A pattern by Müller with two different designs for decorating corners.*

Two further patterns for corners by Müller: these were meant to be used to complete an embroidery.

Two designs for corners in vivid colours by Glüer of Berlin.

Designs with friezes and leaves.

Garlands and butterflies

An old embroidery chart featuring a wide variety of spring flowers.

A late with the same theme as the preceding one but with summer flowers.

Opposite. A butterfly on a branch in the centre of a lovely garland of flowers.
Above. Two plates by Müller with flowers and butterflies.

A butterfly resting on a bouquet of roses at the centre of a frieze. Paris, property of author (embroidery pattern p.176)

Another chart by Müller showing a butterfly in oak leaves.

Two floral patterns by Müller.

Opposite. A floral garland noteworthy for its balanced arrangement. Property of author.
Flower garlands by two different artists.

A small garland with initials at the centre and with small border motifs. Courtesy Textilmuseum, St Gallen (embroidery pattern p.197)

Pleasingly entwined roses and blue campanulas by Muller.

A light blue and gold ribbon wound around a garland by Kratschner (embroideries patterns p.166 and 168)
Following page. A chart by Muller, sadly damaged over the years, still retains its splendid design intact.

Floral Borders

*All the borders in this chapter are very adaptable.
The subjects shown are intended for embroidery use but are not dissimilar to contemporary
decorations on walls, china, inlaid furniture, fabrics and upholstery.
The designs come from a number of different artists. They are all part of the Nowotny Collection.*

132

(embroidery pattern p.200)

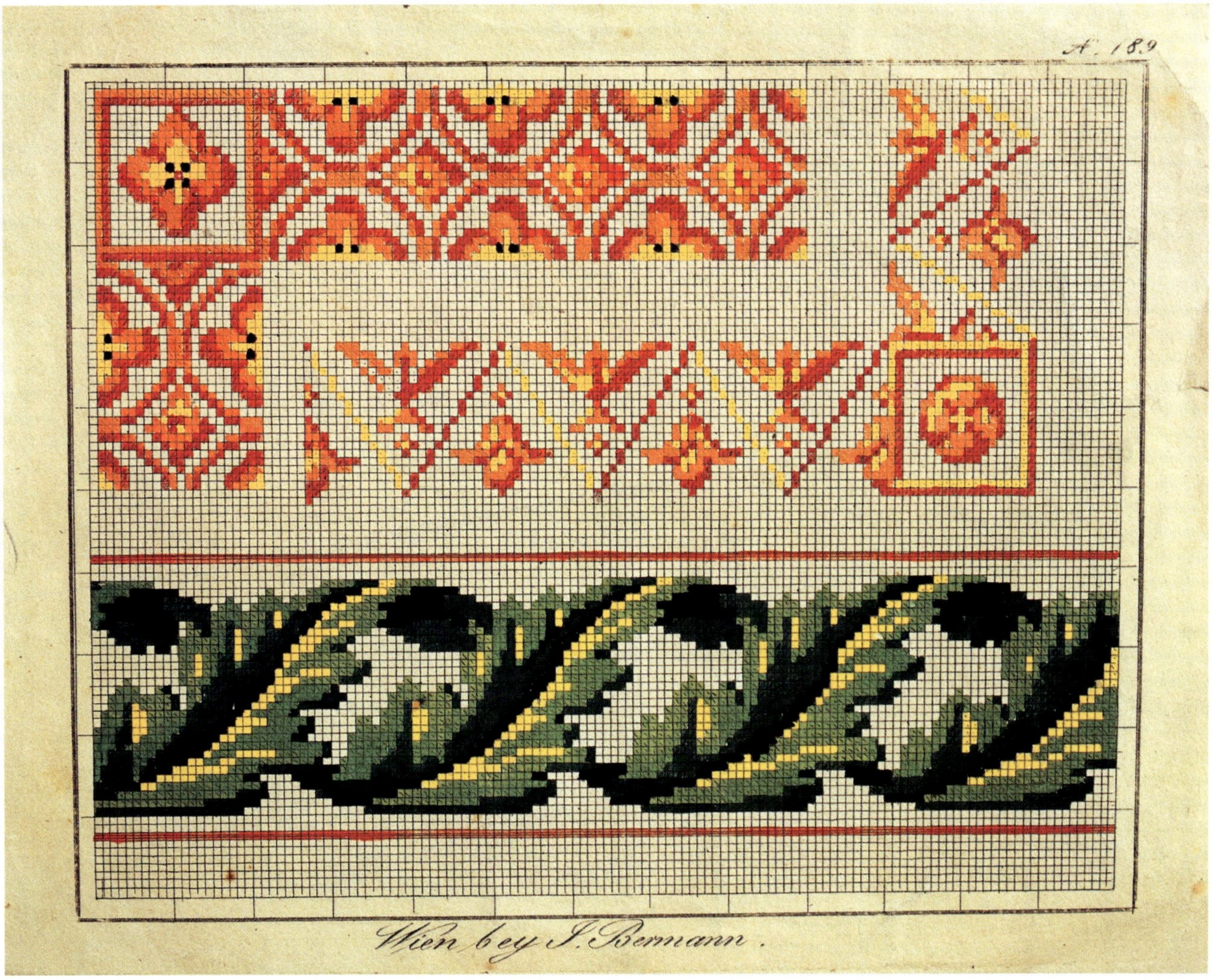
A. 189
Wien bey J. Bermann.

Nº 13
Wien bei H. F. Müller Kunsthändler am Kohlmarkt

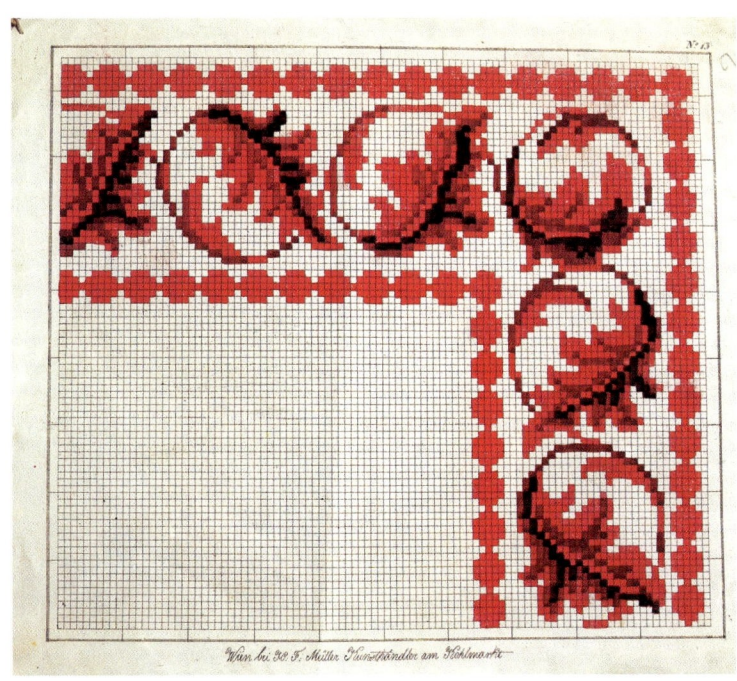

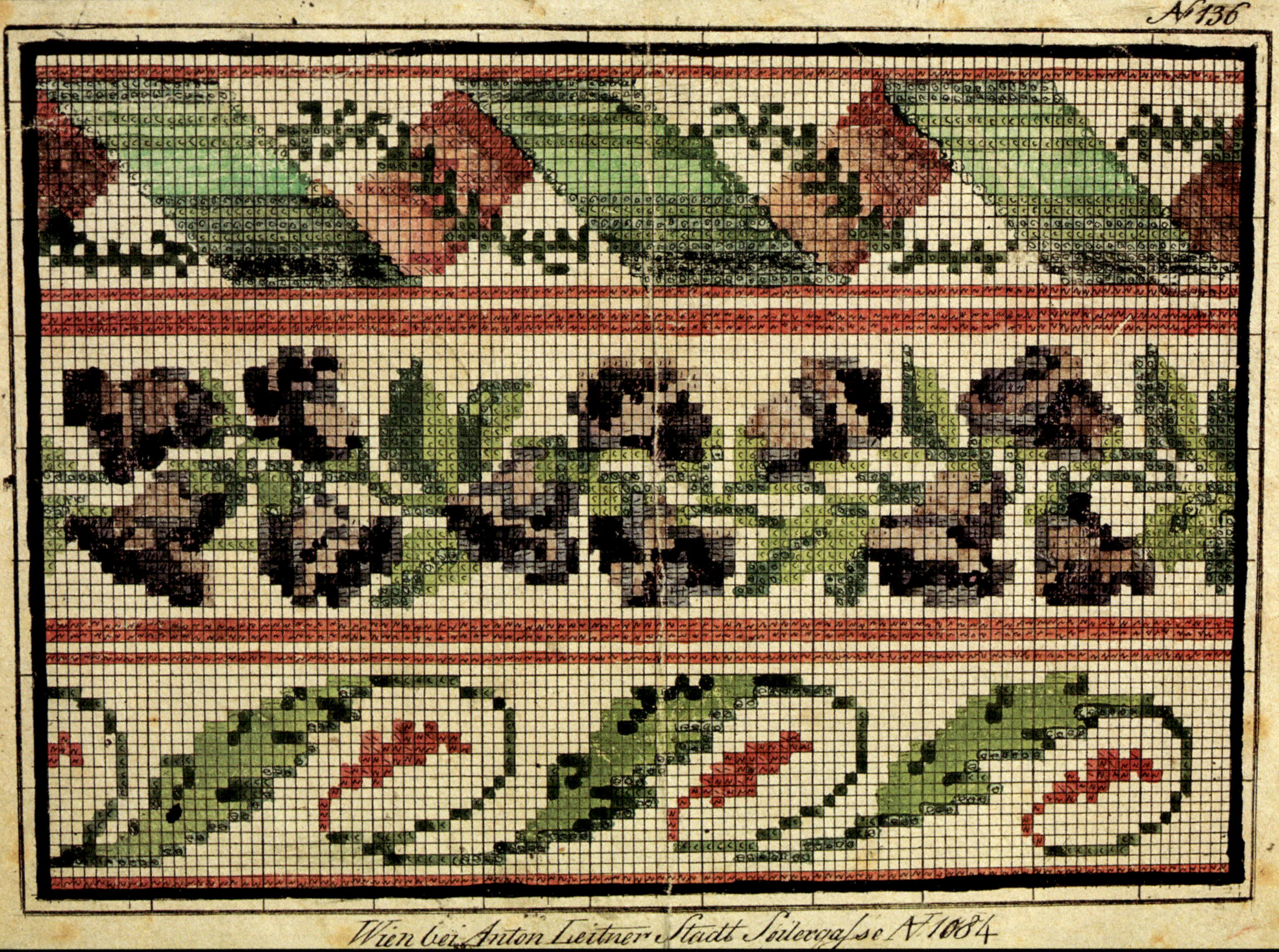
No 136
Wien bei Anton Leitner Stadt Seilergasse No 1084

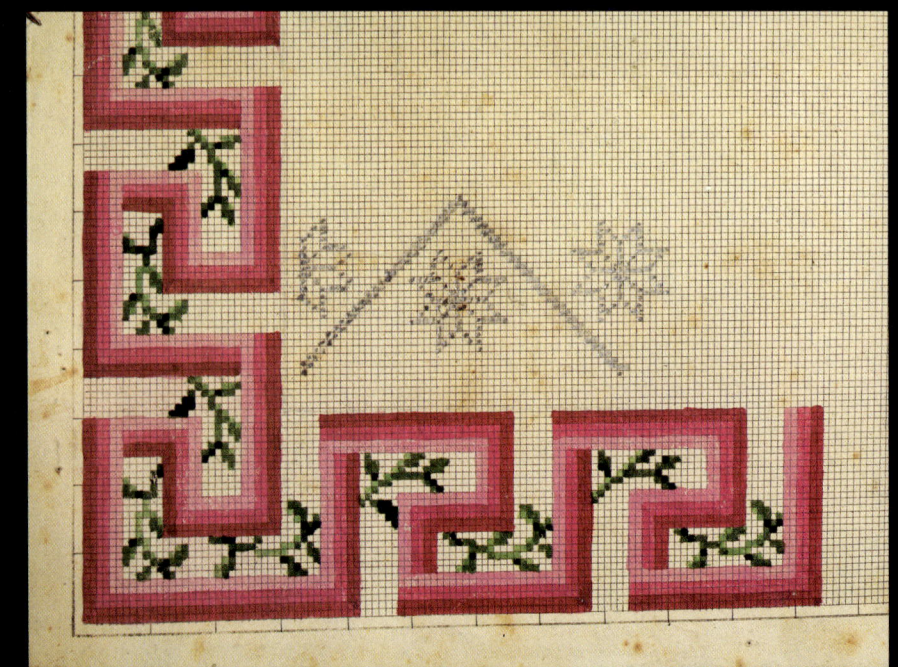

Details

Two plates by Müller with an urn motif (embroidery pattern p.198)

Two plates, one with floral motifs and the other with small designs to be used individually.

Following page. Two very similar designs by Müller showing flowers with elegant friezes in the four corners.

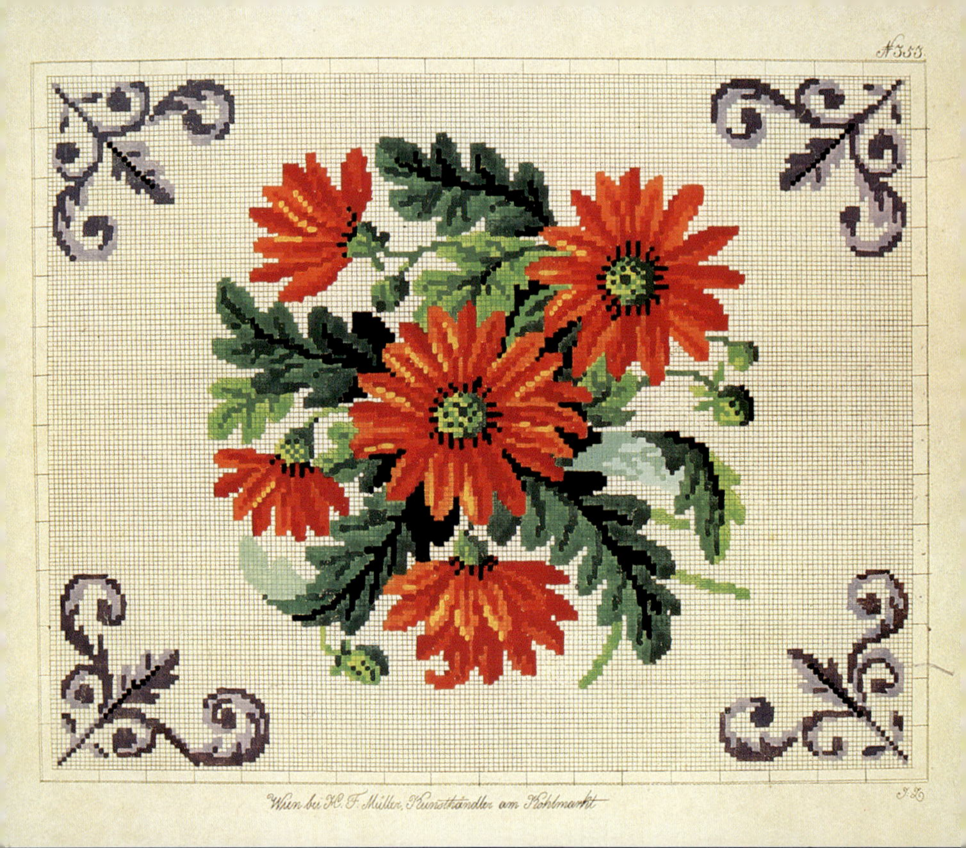

No 353
Wien bei H. F. Müller, Kunsthändler am Kohlmarkt

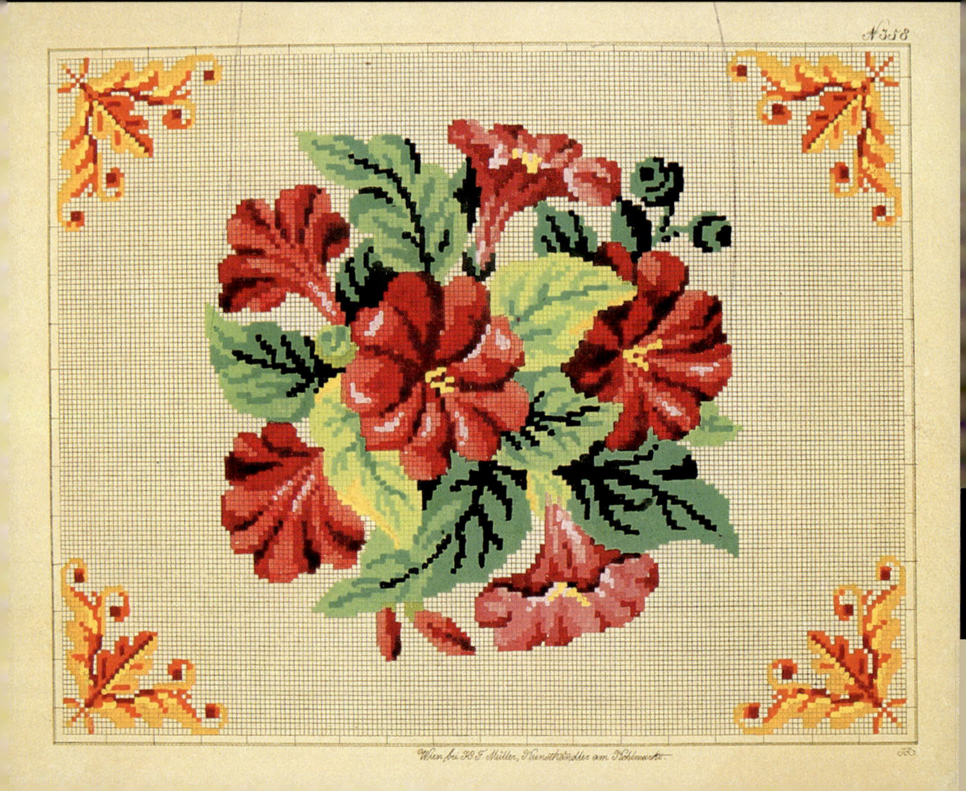

No 358
Wien bei H. F. Müller, Kunsthändler am Kohlmarkt

A huge red rose dominates this chart by Müller.

Classic design with Biedermeier motifs.

Garlands entwined with leaves from different plants are the subject of these two plates by Müller (embroidery pattern p.184)

These two designs and those on the next page show romantic themes much in vogue in the Biedermeier period. (embroidery patterns pp.199, 201).

A graceful little garland bearing the letter 'A' often used as shorthand for 'Amitié' (embroidery pattern p.180)

Upholstery

*Above. A repetitive floral motif pattern for upholstery.
Opposite above. Scattered clover leaves and flowers bound with a light blue ribbon.
Opposite below. Rose shoots entwined on trellis.*

*Above. Small rosebud bouquets against an interesting background in subdued greys by Paterno.
Below. A repetitive pattern suitable for light borders.*

Small objects

Top. A handbag embroidered with beads and crocheted silk border. The word enclosed by the small rose wreath means 'friendship'. The handbag is evidently a gift. Private collection (embroidery pattern p.196)

Above. A small paper box with gilt border and cover decorated with cross stitch embroidery on linen. Courtesy Stickmuster Museum, Celle (embroidery pattern p.200)

Both sides of this handbag embroidered in linen have recurrent Biedermeier period themes: small borders with leaves, a little temple, and flowers. Stickmuster Museum, Celle.

Opposite. A design for a handbag embroidered with delicate-coloured beads. Courtesy Textilmuseum, St Gallen.
Above. A sophisticated design for making a tray to hold various small items. Courtesy Textilmuseum, St Gallen.

Opposite and above. Elegant designs for handbags embroidered with beads. Property of author.

Embroidery and Music

*Musical instruments are the theme of these twelve designs,
a theme that is of particular importance in a book on a nineteenth century
collection from Vienna, the musical capital of the time.*

How to use the Patterns

MORNING DRESS.

Engraven for the Thirty Second Number of New Series of La Belle Assemblee, June 1, 1812.
Printed for John Bell, Southampton Street Strand.

A Lady Embroidering - fashion plate for 'Morning Dress'. From La belle Assemblee, June 1812.
Courtesy Nerylla Taunton, Antique Needlework Tools.

The objects illustrated in the embroidery plates in this book are similar to those used in other branches of the decorative arts such as painting on ceramics, mural decorations, inlay work on furniture, and textile patterns.

However, keeping in mind the original purpose of these design plates and the nature of embroidery and needlework upholstery, I have prepared some embroidery patterns which can be used for doing cross-stitch or petit point embroidery on canvases of various sizes. The yarns suggested are those produced by the firm which is known worldwide by its initials, DMC.

The patterns from pages 166 to 193 are under the two headings of WOOL and MOULINÉ.

WOOL VERSION: These have to be embroidered in petit point on "Penelope" canvas using Colbert wool yarns from DMC and twelve strands of Mouliné cotton from DMC where this has been indicated (M). I have proposed using two different types of yarn, a dull one such as wool and a bright one such as cotton which between them give an impression of greater depth in the embroidered picture by enhancing the play of light.

MOULINÉ VERSION: if a different interpretation is preferred, the same pattern can be done in cross stitch on linen using two or three strands of Mouliné cotton or alternatively done in petit point on unstretched canvas using six strands of Mouliné cotton.

The patterns from pages 194 to 206 are all under the same heading of MOULINÉ.

For these I have suggested using cotton alone since we are dealing with small designs which will retain their full clarity if done in cross stitch on linen or in petit point on unstretched canvas.

Orders for Nowotny Collection embroidery kits should be addressed to:
Ludwig Nowotny
Freisingergasse 4
Petersplats
1010 Vienna,
Austria

Orders for the other embroidery kits should be addressed to:
Raffaella Serena
via Tasso, 11
20123 Milan
Italy

Souvenir • Souvenir • Souvenir • Souvenir

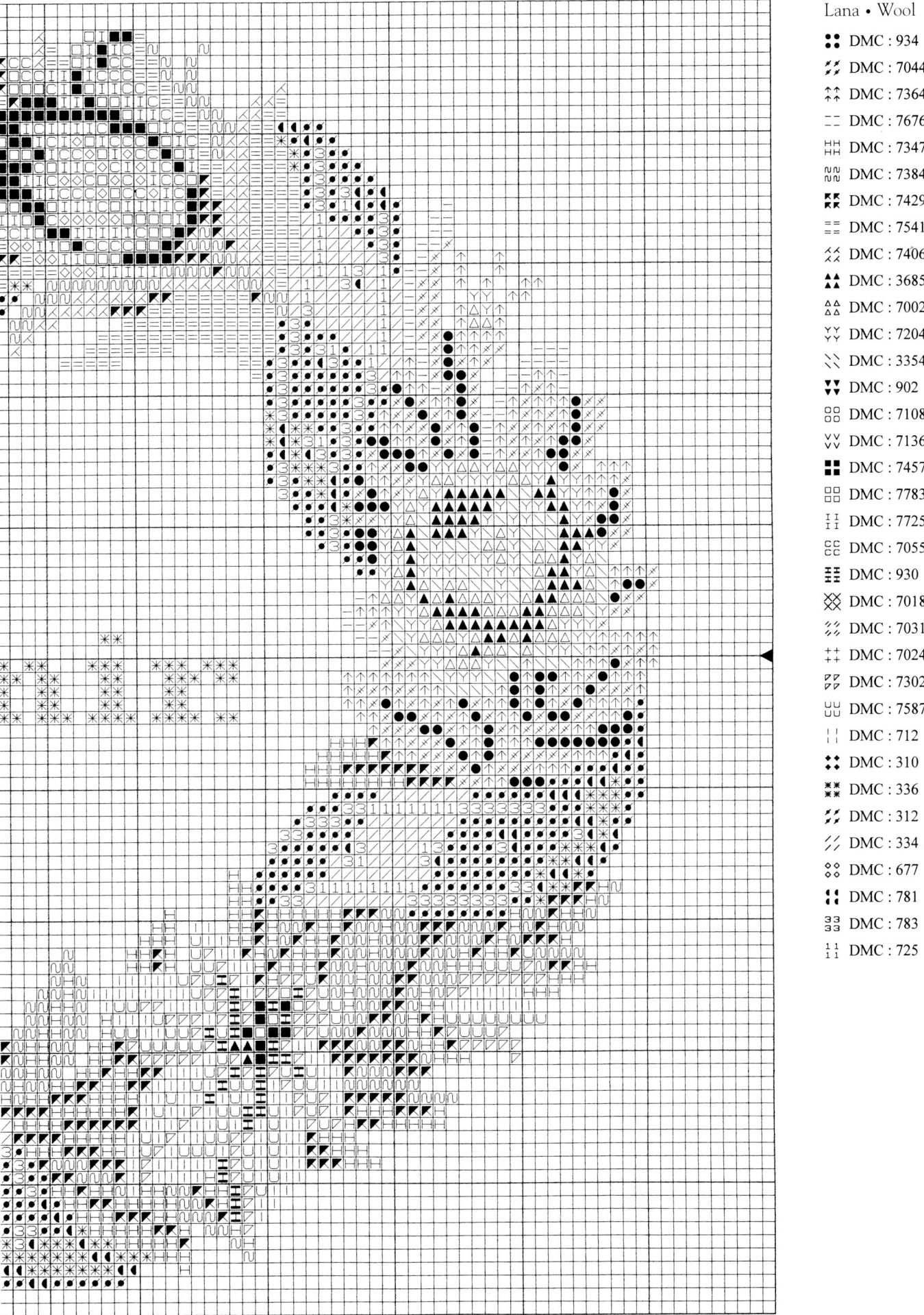

Lana • Wool

- DMC : 934 (M)
- DMC : 7044
- DMC : 7364
- DMC : 7676
- DMC : 7347
- DMC : 7384
- DMC : 7429
- DMC : 7541
- DMC : 7406
- DMC : 3685 (M)
- DMC : 7002
- DMC : 7204
- DMC : 3354 (M)
- DMC : 902 (M)
- DMC : 7108
- DMC : 7136
- DMC : 7457
- DMC : 7783
- DMC : 7725
- DMC : 7055
- DMC : 930 (M)
- DMC : 7018
- DMC : 7031
- DMC : 7024
- DMC : 7302
- DMC : 7587
- DMC : 712 (M)
- DMC : 310 (M)
- DMC : 336 (M)
- DMC : 312 (M)
- DMC : 334 (M)
- DMC : 677 (M)
- DMC : 781 (M)
- DMC : 783 (M)
- DMC : 725 (M)

Souvenir • Souvenir • Souvenir • Souvenir

Mouliné

- :: DMC : 934
- ∥ DMC : 937
- ↑↑ DMC : 470
- = = DMC : 733
- HH DMC : 986
- ∾∾ DMC : 988
- ⊠⊠ DMC : 500
- == DMC : 561
- ⋋⋋ DMC : 502
- ▲▲ DMC : 3685
- △△ DMC : 3687
- YY DMC : 3688
- \\ DMC : 3354
- ▼▼ DMC : 902
- oo DMC : 816
- VV DMC : 309
- ■ DMC : 781
- □□ DMC : 783
- II DMC : 725
- cc DMC : 744
- ≡≡ DMC : 930
- ⊠ DMC : 794
- ∥ DMC : 3747
- ++ DMC : 211
- ▽▽ DMC : 932
- UU DMC : 775
- || DMC : 712
- ●● DMC : 310
- ✻✻ DMC : 336
- ∥ DMC : 312
- // DMC : 334
- ◇◇ DMC : 677

Rose • Roses • Roses • Rosen

Lana • Wool

- :: DMC : 310 (M)
- ▲▲ DMC : 902 (M)
- :: DMC : 7110
- ⁄⁄ DMC : 7138
- ∣∣ DMC : 7136
- ⁄⁄ DMC : 7001
- ✻✻ DMC : 7490
- HH DMC : 7485
- YY DMC : 7473
- ══ DMC : 7359
- ⁄⁄ DMC : 7379
- ○○ DMC : 7044
- ‡‡ DMC : 7364
- ⁄⁄ DMC : 733 (M)
- ✻✻ DMC : 500 (M)
- ∿∿ DMC : 7701
- ⋋⋋ DMC : 502 (M)
- :: DMC : 7004

Mouliné

- :: DMC : 310
- ▲▲ DMC : 902
- :: DMC : 815
- ⁄⁄ DMC : 498
- ∣∣ DMC : 309
- ⁄⁄ DMC : 899
- ✻✻ DMC : 829
- HH DMC : 831
- YY DMC : 833
- ══ DMC : 934
- ⁄⁄ DMC : 935
- ○○ DMC : 937
- ‡‡ DMC : 470
- ⁄⁄ DMC : 734
- ✻✻ DMC : 500
- ∿∿ DMC : 501
- ⋋⋋ DMC : 502
- :: DMC : 776

Piume • Plumes • Feathers • Federn

Lana • Wool

- DMC : 310 (M)
- DMC : 7359
- DMC : 7044
- DMC : 7408
- DMC : 7046
- DMC : 7769
- DMC : 3348 (M)
- DMC : 938 (M)
- DMC : 829 (M)
- DMC : 831 (M)
- DMC : 3051 (M)
- DMC : 7426
- DMC : 7424

- DMC : 7493
- DMC : 7905
- DMC : 7746
- DMC : 7453
- DMC : 814 (M)
- DMC : 7136
- DMC : 7001
- DMC : 7004
- DMC : 818 (M)
- DMC : 7218
- DMC : 7110
- DMC : 7108
- DMC : 7303

- DMC : 920 (M)
- DMC : 7125
- DMC : 976 (M)
- DMC : 783 (M)
- DMC : 676 (M)
- DMC : 823 (M)
- DMC : 7823
- DMC : 7797
- DMC : 798 (M)
- DMC : 7705
- DMC : 7558
- DMC : 762 (M)
- DMC : Blanc (M)

Mouliné

- DMC : 310
- DMC : 934
- DMC : 937
- DMC : 890
- DMC : 3345
- DMC : 3347
- DMC : 3348
- DMC : 938
- DMC : 829
- DMC : 831
- DMC : 3051
- DMC : 3052
- DMC : 3053

- DMC : 3013
- DMC : 3047
- DMC : 712
- DMC : 677
- DMC : 814
- DMC : 309
- DMC : 899
- DMC : 761
- DMC : 818
- DMC : 902
- DMC : 815
- DMC : 817
- DMC : 919

- DMC : 920
- DMC : 921
- DMC : 976
- DMC : 783
- DMC : 676
- DMC : 823
- DMC : 820
- DMC : 797
- DMC : 798
- DMC : 317
- DMC : 415
- DMC : 762
- DMC : Blanc

Violette di Parma • Violettes de Parme • Parma violets • Parmaveilchen

Lana • Wool

- ▲▲ DMC : 823 (M)
- ∷ DMC : 7359
- ∥∥ DMC : 791 (M)
- HH DMC : 7044
- VV DMC : 792 (M)
- YY DMC : 7364
- ∥∥ DMC : 3746(M)
- ∥∥ DMC : 471 (M)
- || DMC : 340 (M)
- ∷ DMC : 7408
- ✲✲ DMC : 921 (M)
- ⊠⊠ DMC : 7046
- ✢✢ DMC : 783 (M)
- ∘∘ DMC : 7045
- —— DMC : 676 (M)
- || DMC : 3348 (M)
- ∷ DMC : 310 (M)

Mouliné

- ▲▲ DMC : 823
- ∷ DMC : 934
- ∥∥ DMC : 791
- HH DMC : 937
- VV DMC : 792
- YY DMC : 470
- ∥∥ DMC : 3746
- ∥∥ DMC : 471
- || DMC : 340
- ∷ DMC : 890
- ✲✲ DMC : 921
- ⊠⊠ DMC : 3345
- ✢✢ DMC : 783
- ∘∘ DMC : 988
- —— DMC : 676
- || DMC : 3348
- ∷ DMC : 310

Campanule • Campanules • Campanulas • Glockemblumen

Lana • Wool

▲▲ DMC : 814 (M)	∷ DMC : 7823	∷ DMC : 310 (M)	
⁄⁄ DMC : 7136	∨∨ DMC : 7797	⋈ DMC : 500 (M)	
◦◦ DMC : 7001	⋌⋌ DMC : 7028	HH DMC : 7379	
YY DMC : 7004	II DMC : 7799	◦◦ DMC : 7320	
⁄⁄ DMC : 7132	⁄⁄ DMC : 318 (M)	⁄⁄ DMC : 7424	
▼▼ DMC : 7023	∣∣ DMC : 415 (M)	✱✱ DMC : 890 (M)	
⊠ DMC : 791 (M)	∘∘ DMC : Blanc (M)	△△ DMC : 7046	
⁄⁄ DMC : 7020	▬▬ DMC : 898 (M)	∧∧ DMC : 7769	
++ DMC : 7019	▫▫ DMC : 420 (M)	↑↑ DMC : 7549	
⟍⟍ DMC : 7031	∨∨ DMC : 783 (M)		
∷ DMC : 939 (M)	═ DMC : 676 (M)		

Mouliné

▲▲ DMC : 814	∷ DMC : 820	∷ DMC : 310
⁄⁄ DMC : 309	∨∨ DMC : 797	⋈ DMC : 500
◦◦ DMC : 899	⋌⋌ DMC : 799	HH DMC : 895
YY DMC : 761	II DMC : 800	◦◦ DMC : 987
⁄⁄ DMC : 818	⁄⁄ DMC : 318	⁄⁄ DMC : 989
▼▼ DMC : 823	∣∣ DMC : 415	✱✱ DMC : 890
⊠ DMC : 791	∘∘ DMC : Blanc	△△ DMC : 3345
⁄⁄ DMC : 792	▬▬ DMC : 898	∧∧ DMC : 3347
++ DMC : 340	▫▫ DMC : 420	↑↑ DMC : 472
⟍⟍ DMC : 3747	∨∨ DMC : 783	
∷ DMC : 939	═ DMC : 676	

Cornucopia • Cornucopia • Cornucopia • Stiefmütterchen

Lana • Wool

:: DMC : 939 (M)	ᵍᵍ DMC : 7393		
ᴷᴷ DMC : 7307	ᴴᴴ DMC : 7364		
✕✕ DMC : 7318	↑↑ DMC : 7583		
ᵇᵇ DMC : 7802	▪▪ DMC : 7695		
\\ DMC : 7301	ᵛᵛ DMC : 7593		
▼▼ DMC : 317 (M)	!! DMC : 7823		
✓✓ DMC : 7620	¹¹ DMC : 561 (M)		
ʸʸ DMC : 7558	³³ DMC : 562 (M)		
== DMC : 7300			
|| DMC : Blanc (M)			
▲▲ DMC : 3371 (M)			
ᵀᵀ DMC : 7467			
−− DMC : 7479			
▶▶ DMC : 7458			
ᴷᴷ DMC : 7446			
∼∼ DMC : 7059			
ᵛᵛ DMC : 7506			
∴∴ DMC : 676 (M)			
▲▲ DMC : 632 (M)			
△△ DMC : 7166			
ᶻᶻ DMC : 7164			
ᵉᵉ DMC : 7179			
ᴵᴵ DMC : 712 (M)			
◀◀ DMC : 902 (M)			
☰☰ DMC : 7110			
▽▽ DMC : 7107			
:: DMC : 7184			
ᵒᵒ DMC : 7010			
ᴾᴾ DMC : 7853			
⨯⨯ DMC : 948 (M)			
⁴⁴ DMC : 791 (M)			
ᶜᶜ DMC : 7019			
// DMC : 7018			
ᵉᵉ DMC : 7797			
⊞⊞ DMC : 809 (M)			
++ DMC : 3713 (M)			
∘∘ DMC : 819 (M)			
■■ DMC : 310 (M)			
✕✕ DMC : 7429			
⊗ DMC : 7327			
++ DMC : 7956			
✓✓ DMC : 7701			
ˢˢ DMC : 7406			
∷∷ DMC : 503 (M)			
✶✶ DMC : 7046			
ᵁᵁ DMC : 7769			
// DMC : 3348 (M)			
▼▼ DMC : 934 (M)			
:: DMC : 7379			
ᴴᴴ DMC : 7044			

Mouliné

:: DMC : 939	ᵍᵍ DMC : 469		
ᴷᴷ DMC : 336	ᴴᴴ DMC : 470		
✕✕ DMC : 312	↑↑ DMC : 471		
ᵇᵇ DMC : 334	▪▪ DMC : 930		
\\ DMC : 3325	ᵛᵛ DMC : 931		
▼▼ DMC : 317	!! DMC : 820		
✓✓ DMC : 318	¹¹ DMC : 561		
ʸʸ DMC : 415	³³ DMC : 562		
== DMC : 762			
|| DMC : Blanc			
▲▲ DMC : 3371			
ᵀᵀ DMC : 898			
−− DMC : 801			
▶▶ DMC : 300			
ᴷᴷ DMC : 301			
∼∼ DMC : 435			
ᵛᵛ DMC : 729			
∴∴ DMC : 676			
▲▲ DMC : 632			
△△ DMC : 3772			
ᶻᶻ DMC : 3773			
ᵉᵉ DMC : 3774			
ᴵᴵ DMC : 712			
◀◀ DMC : 902			
☰☰ DMC : 815			
▽▽ DMC : 326			
:: DMC : 3777			
ᵒᵒ DMC : 3778			
ᴾᴾ DMC : 3779			
⨯⨯ DMC : 948			
⁴⁴ DMC : 791			
ᶜᶜ DMC : 793			
// DMC : 794			
ᵉᵉ DMC : 797			
⊞⊞ DMC : 809			
++ DMC : 3713			
∘∘ DMC : 819			
■■ DMC : 310			
✕✕ DMC : 500			
⊗ DMC : 991			
++ DMC : 992			
✓✓ DMC : 501			
ˢˢ DMC : 502			
∷∷ DMC : 503			
✶✶ DMC : 3345			
ᵁᵁ DMC : 3347			
// DMC : 3348			
▼▼ DMC : 934			
:: DMC : 935			
ᴴᴴ DMC : 937			

Cuscino con farfalla • Coussin avec papillon • Cushion with butterfly • Kissen mit Schmetterling

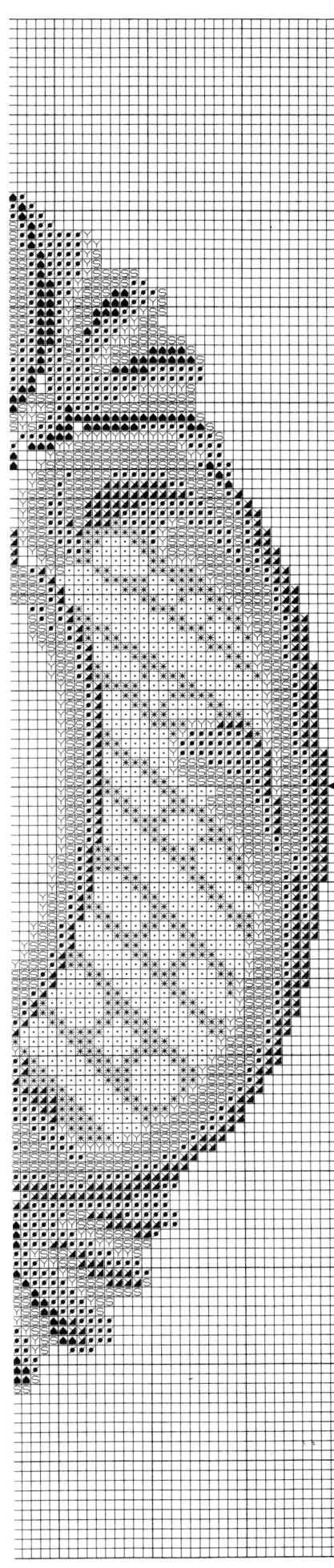

Lana • Wool

- ⹁⹁ DMC : 309 (M)
- YY DMC : 676 (M)
- LL DMC : 7505
- :: DMC : 7355
- ⁄⁄ DMC : 7353
- ⱽⱽ DMC : 7761
- ⁄⁄ DMC : 471 (M)
- ✕✕ DMC : 829 (M)
- ss DMC : 7504
- ɴɴ DMC : 7620
- ++ DMC : 7336
- ++ DMC : 7768
- °° DMC : 3779 (M)
- ⊥⊥ DMC : 7320
- ☐☐ DMC : 7401
- ⊙⊙ DMC : 7759
- •• DMC : 7207
- ⁄⁄ DMC : 7770
- KK DMC : 7428
- :::: DMC : 988 (M)
- ▲▲ DMC : 839 (M)
- ✴✴ DMC : 312 (M)
- ⲏⲏ DMC : 7138
- ▼▼ DMC : 310 (M)
- ▲▲ DMC : 7890
- KK DMC : 7429
- ⱽⱽ DMC : 7375
- HH DMC : 7713
- ⊤⊤ DMC : 7139

177

Viole • Violettes • Violets • Veilchen

Lana • Wool	Mouliné
●● DMC : 500 (M)	●● DMC : 500
✕✕ DMC : 7541	✕✕ DMC : 561
⊓⊓ DMC : 7320	⊓⊓ DMC : 987
✱✱ DMC : 934 (M)	✱✱ DMC : 934
⧻⧻ DMC : 7046	⧻⧻ DMC : 3345
∕∕ DMC : 7044	∕∕ DMC : 937
⌐⌐ DMC : 7364	⌐⌐ DMC : 470
══ DMC : 7676	══ DMC : 733
▲▲ DMC : 7023	▲▲ DMC : 823
▬▬ DMC : 791 (M)	▬▬ DMC : 791
∕∕ DMC : 7022	∕∕ DMC : 3746
∕∕ DMC : 7241	∕∕ DMC : 340
TT DMC : 7019	TT DMC : 793
⊗⊗ DMC : 7018	⊗⊗ DMC : 794
VV DMC : 7031	VV DMC : 3747
⎮⎮ DMC : 3756 (M)	⎮⎮ DMC : 3756
◇◇ DMC : 7025	◇◇ DMC : 209
++ DMC : 211 (M)	++ DMC : 211
▪▪ DMC : 7479	▪▪ DMC : 801
▫▫ DMC : 7457	▫▫ DMC : 434
⌐⌐ DMC : 7783	⌐⌐ DMC : 783
⫽⫽ DMC : 7725	⫽⫽ DMC : 725
YY DMC : 744 (M)	YY DMC : 744
♥♥ DMC : 7391	♥♥ DMC : 730
⌂⌂ DMC : 7474	⌂⌂ DMC : 832
┴┴ DMC : 834 (M)	┴┴ DMC : 834

Petunie • Pétunias • Petunias • Petunien

Lana • Wool

- ▲▲ DMC : 7199
- △△ DMC : 7002
- == DMC : 7204
- ✗✗ DMC : 7133
- ┆┆ DMC : 3713 (M)
- ∽∽ DMC : 783 (M)
- ✗✗ DMC : 725 (M)
- ✱✱ DMC : 797 (M)
- •• DMC : 7429
- ++ DMC : 7701
- ∕∕ DMC : 992 (M)
- ╪╪ DMC : 7541
- ⊗⊗ DMC : 7542
- ∨∨ DMC : 563 (M)

Mouliné

- ▲▲ DMC : 3685
- △△ DMC : 3687
- == DMC : 3688
- ✗✗ DMC : 3326
- ┆┆ DMC : 3713
- ∽∽ DMC : 783
- ✗✗ DMC : 725
- ✱✱ DMC : 797
- •• DMC : 500
- ++ DMC : 991
- ∕∕ DMC : 992
- ╪╪ DMC : 561
- ⊗⊗ DMC : 562
- ∨∨ DMC : 563

Ortensie • Hortensias • Hydrangeas • Hortensien

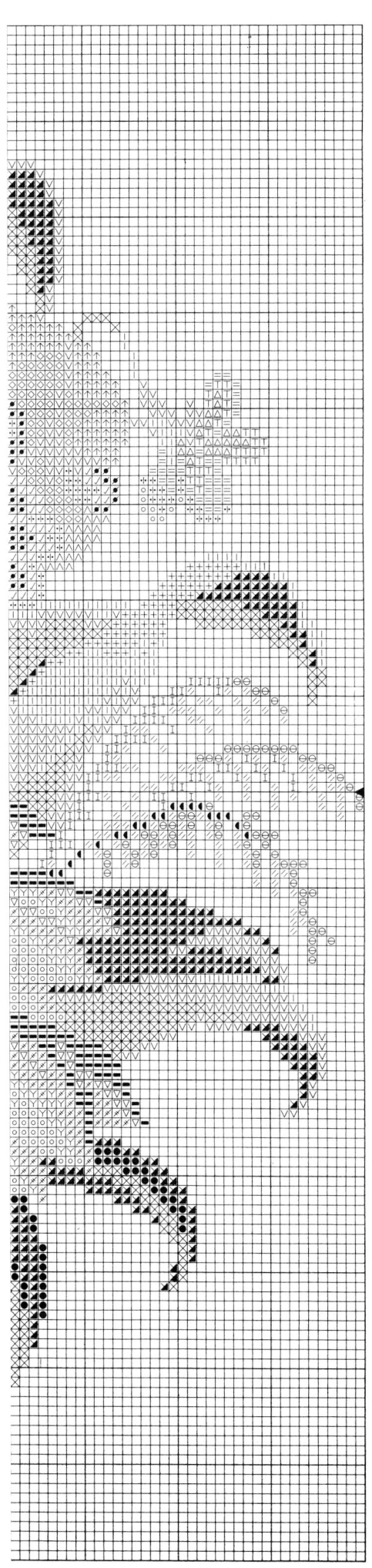

Lana • Wool	Mouliné
:: DMC : 310 (M)	:: DMC : 310
vv DMC : 7359	vv DMC : 934
:: DMC : 7396	:: DMC : 520
8° DMC : 7376	8° DMC : 3363
⋈⋈ DMC : 7361	⋈⋈ DMC : 3364
\\ DMC : 7549	\\ DMC : 472
^^ DMC : 522 (M)	^^ DMC : 522
↑↑ DMC : 523 (M)	↑↑ DMC : 523
⋇⋇ DMC : 7329	⋇⋇ DMC : 924
⊗⊗ DMC : 7702	⊗⊗ DMC : 3768
vv DMC : 7703	vv DMC : 926
|| DMC : 7704	|| DMC : 927
++ DMC : 7321	++ DMC : 928
!! DMC : 898 (M)	!! DMC : 898
°° DMC : 434 (M)	°° DMC : 434
∥∥ DMC : 435 (M)	∥∥ DMC : 435
II DMC : 437 (M)	II DMC : 437
✻✻ DMC : 921 (M)	✻✻ DMC : 921
▫▫ DMC : 783 (M)	▫▫ DMC : 783
≺≺ DMC : 676 (M)	≺≺ DMC : 676
TT DMC : 823 (M)	TT DMC : 823
⁝⁝ DMC : 797 (M)	⁝⁝ DMC : 797
ΔΔ DMC : 7029	ΔΔ DMC : 798
TT DMC : 7798	TT DMC : 799
// DMC : 7799	// DMC : 800
== DMC : 3753 (M)	== DMC : 3753
°° DMC : Blanc (M)	°° DMC : Blanc
▬▬ DMC : 3787 (M)	▬▬ DMC : 3787
∇∇ DMC : 7390	∇∇ DMC : 3022
∥∥ DMC : 524 (M)	∥∥ DMC : 524
YY DMC : 7411	YY DMC : 3024
// DMC : 7033	// DMC : 793
≡≡ DMC : 7028	≡≡ DMC : 794
// DMC : 7018	// DMC : 341
++ DMC : 3747(M)	++ DMC : 3747

Rami intrecciati • Branches entrecroisées • Intertwined branches • Geflochtene Zweige

Viole del pensiero • Pensées • Pansies • Vergissmeinnicht

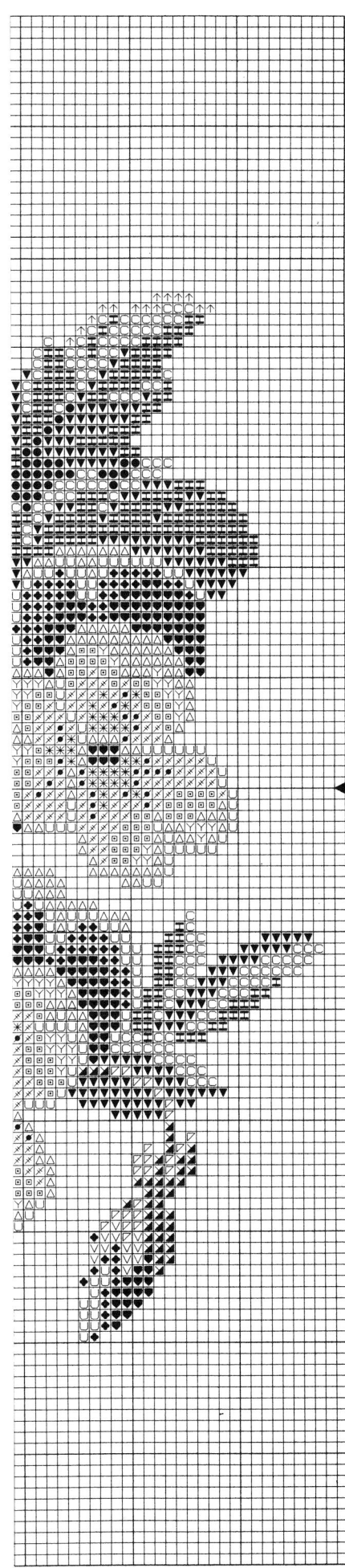

Lana • Wool	Mouliné
∷ DMC : 310 (M)	∷ DMC : 310
∷ DMC : 319 (M)	∷ DMC : 319
ⱽⱽ DMC : 7359	ⱽⱽ DMC : 934
☰ DMC : 7044	☰ DMC : 937
cc DMC : 7364	cc DMC : 470
↑↑ DMC : 7583	↑↑ DMC : 471
\\ DMC : 472 (M)	\\ DMC : 472
⊤⊤ DMC : 7408	⊤⊤ DMC : 890
▱▱ DMC : 7046	▱▱ DMC : 3345
ᵛᵛ DMC : 7769	ᵛᵛ DMC : 988
✖✖ DMC : 7429	✖✖ DMC : 500
⊗ DMC : 7541	⊗ DMC : 561
‡‡ DMC : 7406	‡‡ DMC : 502
∥∥ DMC : 504 (M)	∥∥ DMC : 504
▬▬ DMC : 7447	▬▬ DMC : 918
⁄⁄ DMC : 7125	⁄⁄ DMC : 921
⁄⁄ DMC : 7214	⁄⁄ DMC : 922
═ DMC : 783 (M)	═ DMC : 783
⁄⁄ DMC : 7725	⁄⁄ DMC : 725
▫▫ DMC : 7055	▫▫ DMC : 744
✱✱ DMC : 300 (M)	✱✱ DMC : 300
⁄⁄ DMC : 7059	⁄⁄ DMC : 435
◇◇ DMC : 7144	◇◇ DMC : 437
YY DMC : 7746	YY DMC : 712
∘∘ DMC : Blanc	∘∘ DMC : Blanc
II DMC : 761 (M)	II DMC : 761
▲▲ DMC : 7119	▲▲ DMC : 902
▫▫ DMC : 7110	▫▫ DMC : 815
∧∧ DMC : 7108	∧∧ DMC : 498
♥♥ DMC : 7023	♥♥ DMC : 823
∷ DMC : 7020	∷ DMC : 791
UU DMC : 7019	UU DMC : 793
∧∧ DMC : 341 (M)	∧∧ DMC : 341

Convolvoli • Convolvulus • Convolvulus • Winden

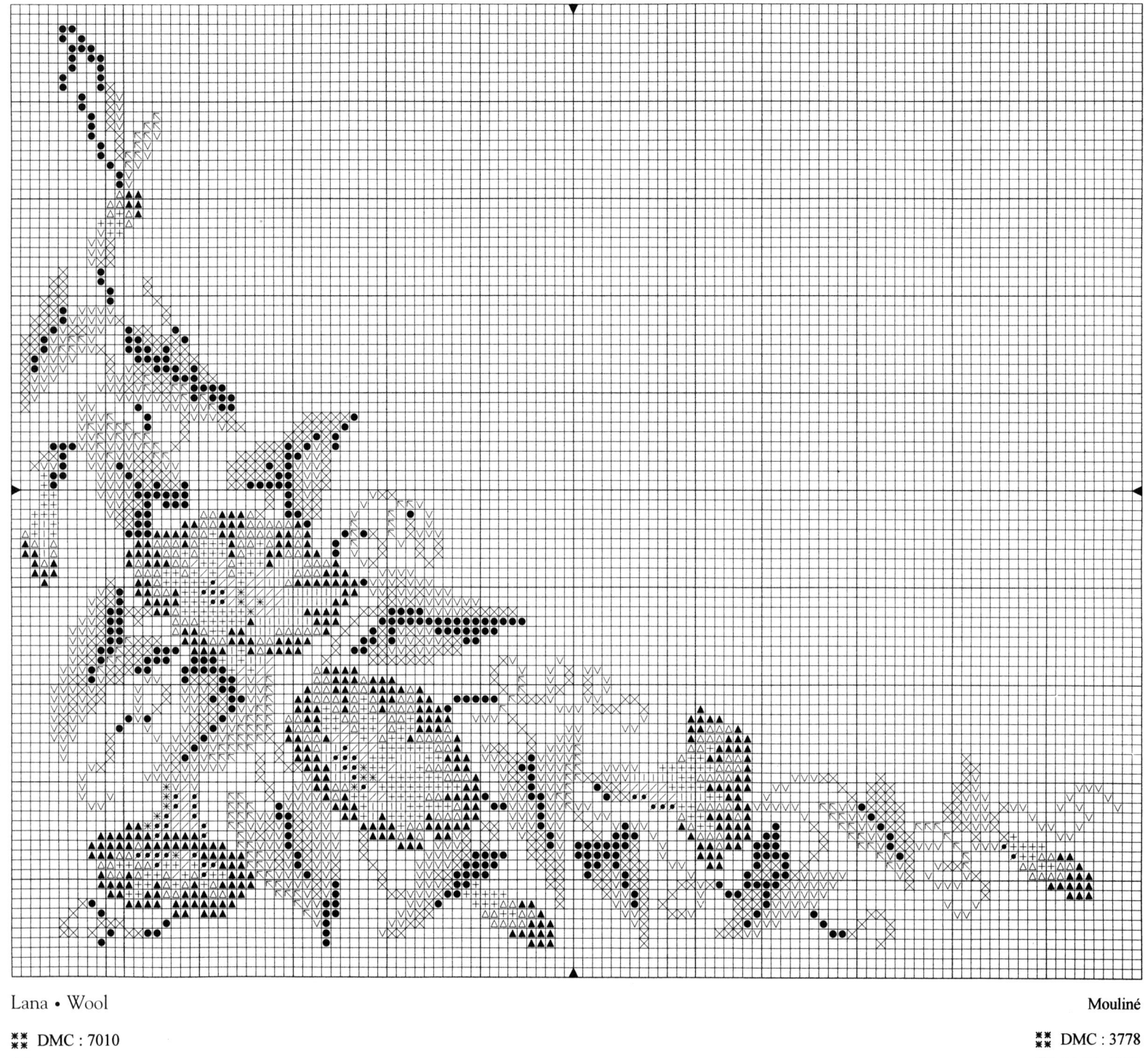

Lana • Wool

- ✳✳ DMC : 7010
- ∥∥ DMC : 7853
- ∥∥ DMC : 3774 (M)
- ▲▲ DMC : 7030
- △△ DMC : 7028
- ++ DMC : 7031
- ∥∥ DMC : Blanc (M)
- •• DMC : 934 (M)
- ⊠ DMC : 7044
- vv DMC : 7364
- ⥀⥀ DMC : 7676

Mouliné

- ✳✳ DMC : 3778
- ∥∥ DMC : 3779
- ∥∥ DMC : 3774
- ▲▲ DMC : 312
- △△ DMC : 799
- ++ DMC : 3747
- ∥∥ DMC : Blanc
- •• DMC : 934
- ⊠ DMC : 937
- vv DMC : 470
- ⥀⥀ DMC : 733

Rosa • Rose • Rose • Rose

Lana • Wool	Mouliné
▲▲ DMC : 934 (M)	▲▲ DMC : 934
ᵛᵛ DMC : 7044	ᵛᵛ DMC : 937
∣∣ DMC : 7548	∣∣ DMC : 471
●● DMC : 3685 (M)	●● DMC : 3685
∥∥ DMC : 7002	∥∥ DMC : 3687
∥∥ DMC : 7204	∥∥ DMC : 3688
∷ DMC : 3713 (M)	∷ DMC : 3713
⊠ DMC : 7468	⊠ DMC : 938
∥∥ DMC : 801 (M)	∥∥ DMC : 801

Bordo di rose • Bordure des roses • Border of roses • Rosenbordüre

Lana • Wool

∷	DMC : Blanc (M)	ᖴᖴ	DMC : 7364
∥	DMC : 7132	∖∖	DMC : 7549
∦	DMC : 7003	↑↑	DMC : 7769
ᵞᵞ	DMC : 7001	∥	DMC : 7320
ᵒᵒ	DMC : 7136	▲▲	DMC : 890 (M)
ᵀᵀ	DMC : 7110	♥♥	DMC : 310 (M)
••	DMC : 902 (M)	✻✻	DMC : 7429
⊞⊞	DMC : 300 (M)	∥	DMC : 7541
□□	DMC : 400 (M)	ᵛᵛ	DMC : 7542
◇◇	DMC : 7474	++	DMC : 563 (M)
∦	DMC : 7490	==	DMC : 7468
■■	DMC : 3371 (M)		

Mouliné

- ∷ DMC : Blanc
- ∕∕ DMC : 3713
- ∕∕ DMC : 3326
- YY DMC : 335
- ◻◻ DMC : 326
- TT DMC : 815
- •• DMC : 902
- ⊞⊞ DMC : 300
- ◻◻ DMC : 400
- ◊◊ DMC : 832
- ∕∕ DMC : 829
- ■■ DMC : 3371
- ⊟⊟ DMC : 470
- ∖∖ DMC : 472
- ↑↑ DMC : 989
- ∕∕ DMC : 987
- ▲▲ DMC : 890
- ♥♥ DMC : 310
- ✱✱ DMC : 500
- ∕∕ DMC : 561
- VV DMC : 562
- ✝✝ DMC : 563
- ▬▬ DMC : 938

191

Fiori con nastro • Fleurs avec ruban • Flowers with ribbon • Blumen mit Band

Lana • Wool

▬▬ DMC : 791	∕∕ DMC : 436	═ DMC : 7404	H H DMC : 7573	◦◦ DMC : 7107	⊠⊠ DMC : 7004	▫▫ DMC : 434
≡≡ DMC : 793	│ │ DMC : 676	∕∕ DMC : 7385	▷▷ DMC : 7676	∟∟ DMC : 7005	△△ DMC : 7003	▪▪ DMC : 801
∕∕ DMC : 794	▲▲ DMC : 500	∼∼ DMC : 7384	\\ DMC : 7474	⟨⟨ DMC : 7012	⅃⅃ DMC : 818	◦◦ DMC : 7031
◊◊ DMC : 3747	∕∕ DMC : 7541	╪╪ DMC : 7771	•• DMC : 902	▼▼ DMC : 326	∴∴ DMC : Blanc	⅂⅂ DMC : 7402
∨∨ DMC : 762	∨∨ DMC : 7406	┬┬ DMC : 935	⟨⟨ DMC : 7110	≣≣ DMC : 7001	╪╪ DMC : 7568	∧∧ DMC : 7772

Mouliné

▬▬ DMC : 791	∕∕ DMC : 436	═ DMC : 503	H H DMC : 732	◦◦ DMC : 3328	⊠⊠ DMC : 776	▫▫ DMC : 434
≡≡ DMC : 793	│ │ DMC : 676	∕∕ DMC : 987	▷▷ DMC : 733	∟∟ DMC : 760	△△ DMC : 3713	▪▪ DMC : 801
∕∕ DMC : 794	▲▲ DMC : 500	∼∼ DMC : 989	\\ DMC : 834	⟨⟨ DMC : 761	⅃⅃ DMC : 818	⅂⅂ DMC : 504
◊◊ DMC : 3747	∕∕ DMC : 561	╪╪ DMC : 471	•• DMC : 902	▼▼ DMC : 326	∴∴ DMC : Blanc	∧∧ DMC : 472
∨∨ DMC : 762	∨∨ DMC : 502	┬┬ DMC : 935	⟨⟨ DMC : 815	≣≣ DMC : 961	╪╪ DMC : 3756	

Pastorella • Bergère • Shepherdess • Schäferin

Mouliné

- DMC : 3773
- DMC : 3774
- DMC : 3685
- DMC : 3687
- DMC : 3688
- DMC : 3689
- DMC : Blanc
- DMC : 3747
- DMC : 3371
- DMC : 938
- DMC : 898
- DMC : 420
- DMC : 436
- DMC : 640
- DMC : 3032
- DMC : 3782
- DMC : 644
- DMC : 712
- DMC : 3721
- DMC : 223
- DMC : 224
- DMC : 934
- DMC : 936
- DMC : 937
- DMC : 470
- DMC : 3347
- DMC : 3348
- DMC : 3012
- DMC : 3013
- DMC : 520
- DMC : 3363
- DMC : 3364
- DMC : 935
- DMC : 3051
- DMC : 3052
- DMC : 3053
- DMC : 501
- DMC : 502

Borsetta • Petit sac • Small bag • Täschchen

Mouliné

▪▪	DMC : 311	⊠⊠	DMC : 581
ʏʏ	DMC : 826	ᴴᴴ	DMC : 733
╲╲	DMC : 827	⇃⇃	DMC : 3346
ᵥᵥ	DMC : 799	↓↓	DMC : 3347
▬▬	DMC : 800	∣∣	DMC : 3348
●●	DMC : 3685	┼┼	DMC : 801
⁄⁄	DMC : 3731	::	DMC : 780
⁄⁄	DMC : 3733	⊖⊖	DMC : 783
∕∕	DMC : 761	╈╈	DMC : 743
∘∘	DMC : 948	∧∧	DMC : 680
▲▲	DMC : 936	══	DMC : 676

Ghirlandina con iniziale • Petite guirlande avec intiale • Small garland with initial • Kleine Girlande mit Initiale

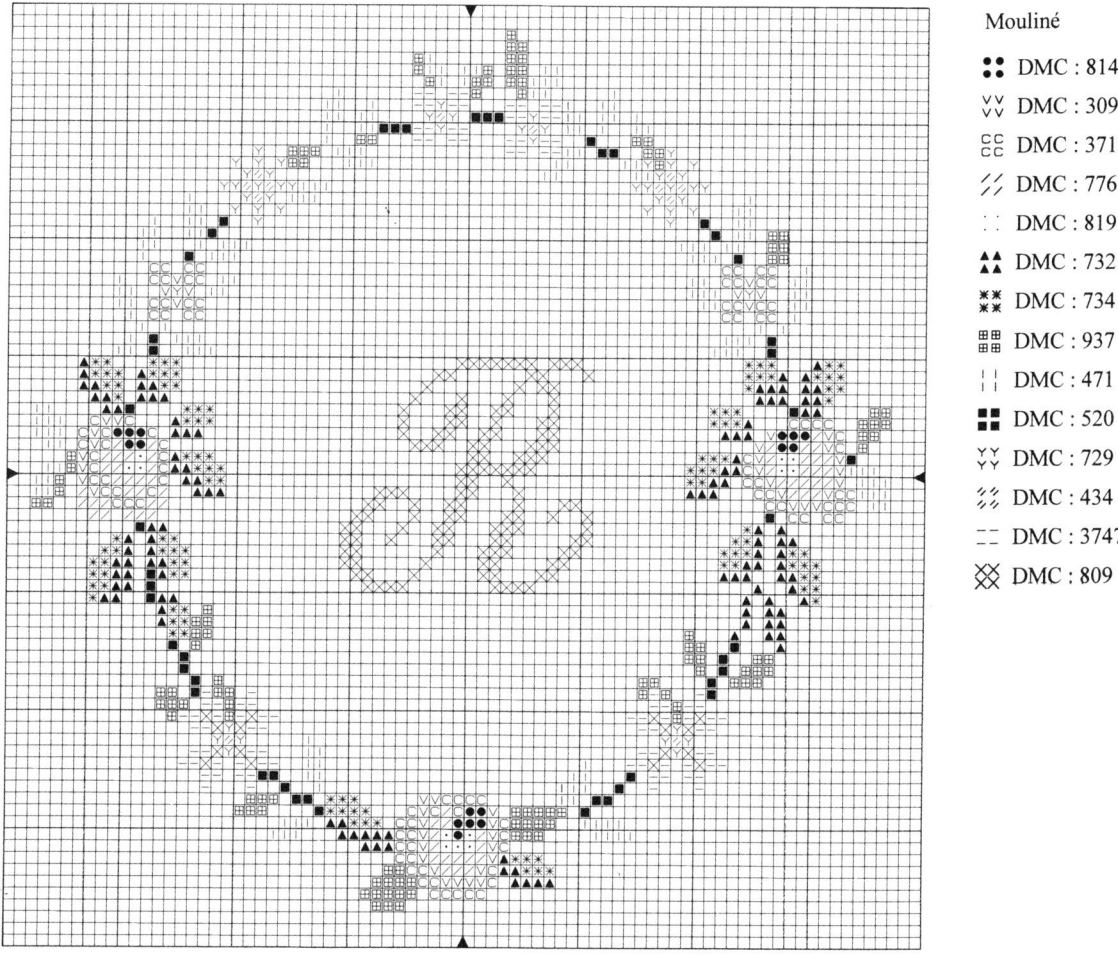

Mouliné
- ∷ DMC : 814
- ᵛᵛ DMC : 309
- ᶜᶜ DMC : 3712
- ∕∕ DMC : 776
- ∷ DMC : 819
- ▲▲ DMC : 732
- ✱✱ DMC : 734
- ⊞⊞ DMC : 937
- ┆┆ DMC : 471
- ■■ DMC : 520
- ᵧᵧ DMC : 729
- ∕∕ DMC : 434
- ⁼⁼ DMC : 3747
- ✕✕ DMC : 809

Coroncina • Petite couronne • Coronet • Kränzlein

Mouliné
- ∷ DMC : 315
- ᵧᵧ DMC : 316
- ∕∕ DMC : 778
- ⁼⁼ DMC : 500
- ∕∕ DMC : 367
- ∷ DMC : 368
- ▫▫ DMC : 801
- ▲▲ DMC : 3750
- ᵛᵛ DMC : 931
- ┆┆ DMC : 3752

Arpa • Harpe • Harp • Harfe

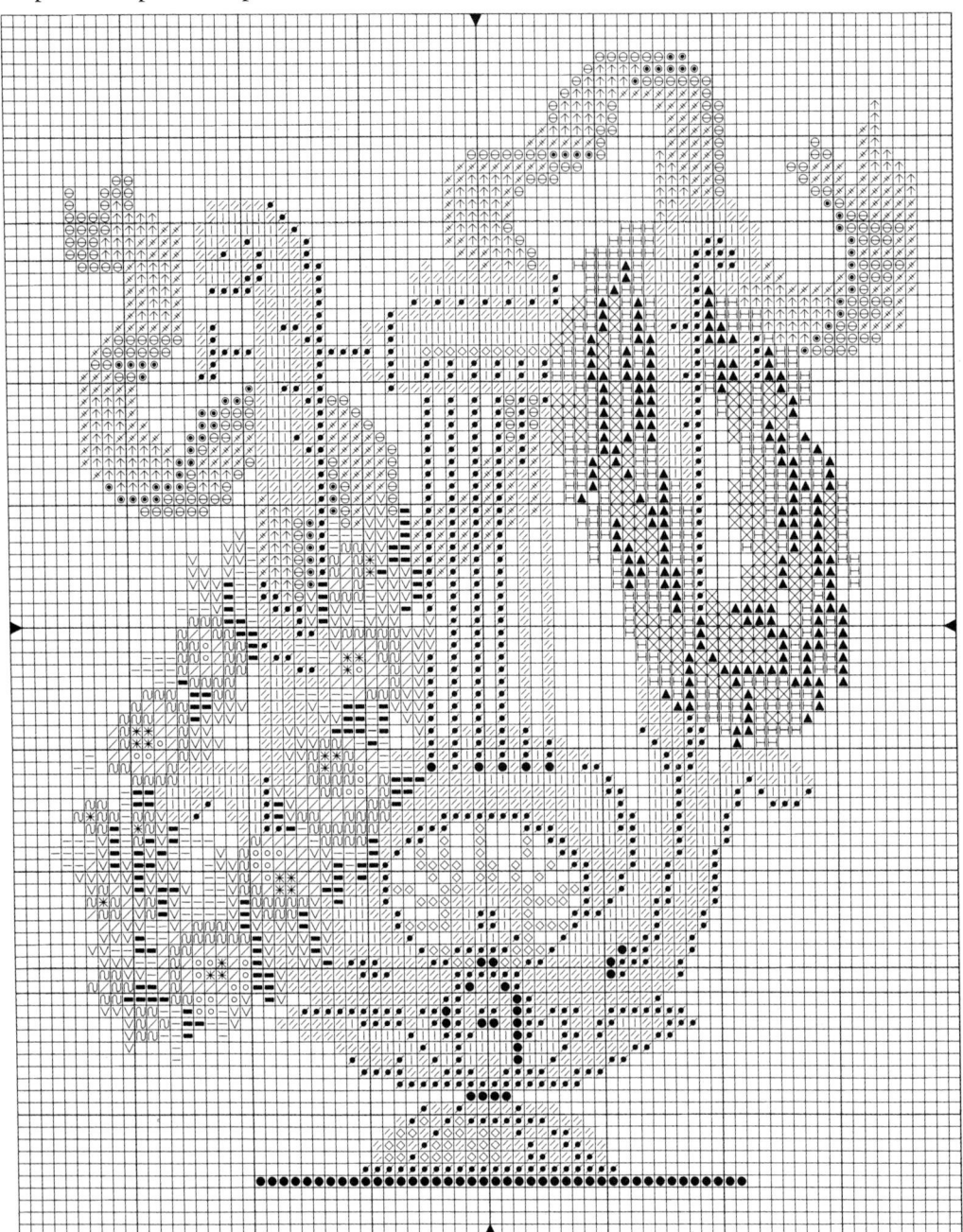

Mouliné

- :: DMC : 938
- ∕∕ DMC : 918
- ∕∕ DMC : 781
- ∘∘ DMC : 783
- | | DMC : 725
- ▲▲ DMC : 890
- HH DMC : 987
- ⊠ DMC : 989
- -- DMC : 895
- VV DMC : 3346
- == DMC : 471
- ✳✳ DMC : 3685
- ωω DMC : 3350
- ∕∕ DMC : 3733
- ∘∘ DMC : 963
- :: DMC : 796
- ∘∘ DMC : 798
- ∕∕ DMC : 799
- ↑↑ DMC : 800

Ancora • Ancre • Anchor • Anker

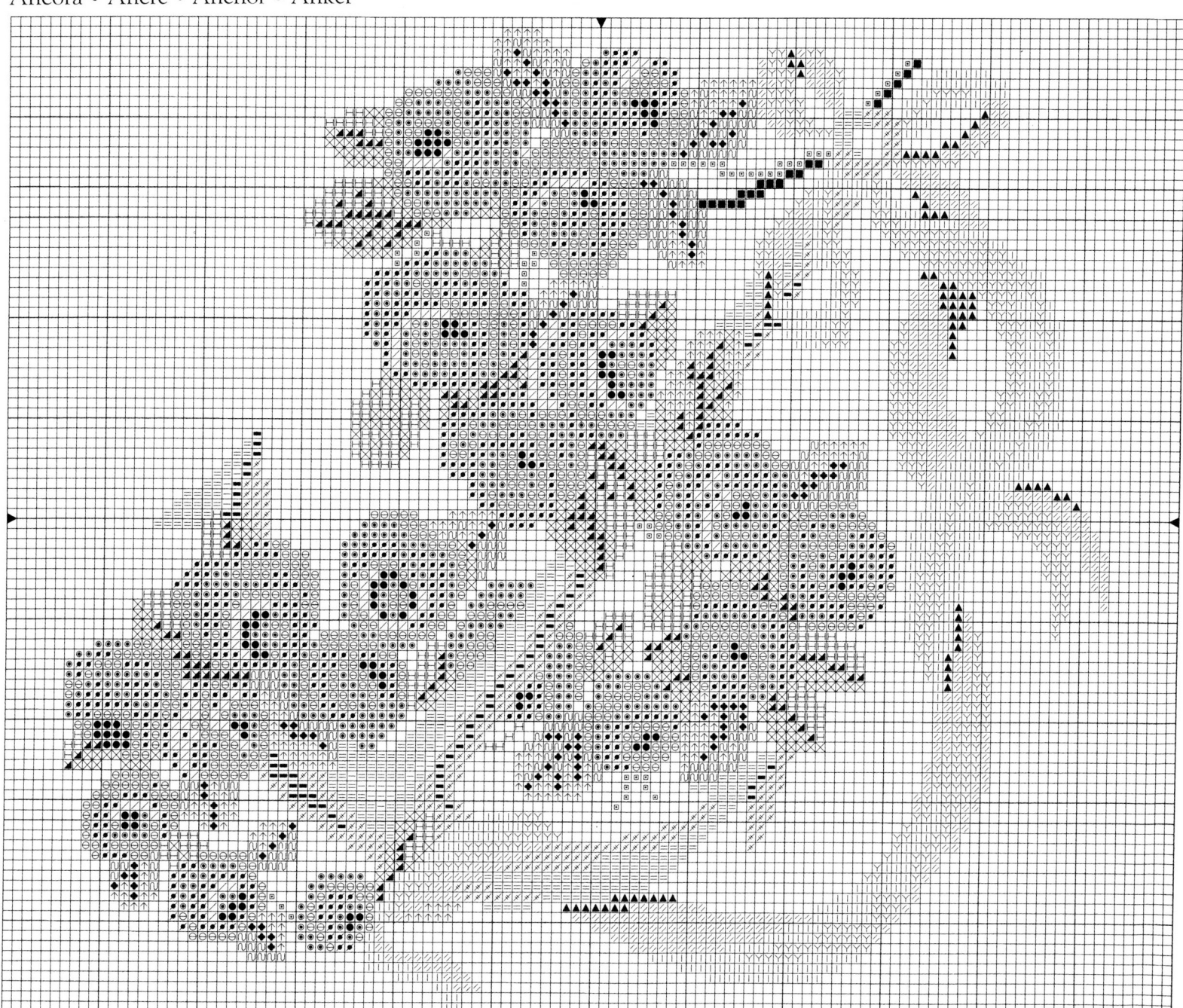

Mouliné

- DMC : 3685
- DMC : 3350
- DMC : 3731
- DMC : 3733
- DMC : 963
- DMC : 801
- DMC : 434
- DMC : 370
- DMC : 729
- DMC : 744
- DMC : 746
- DMC : 820
- DMC : 797
- DMC : 798
- DMC : 799
- DMC : 934
- DMC : 937
- DMC : 470
- DMC : 895
- DMC : 3346
- DMC : 3348

Scettro • Sceptre • Sceptre • Zepter

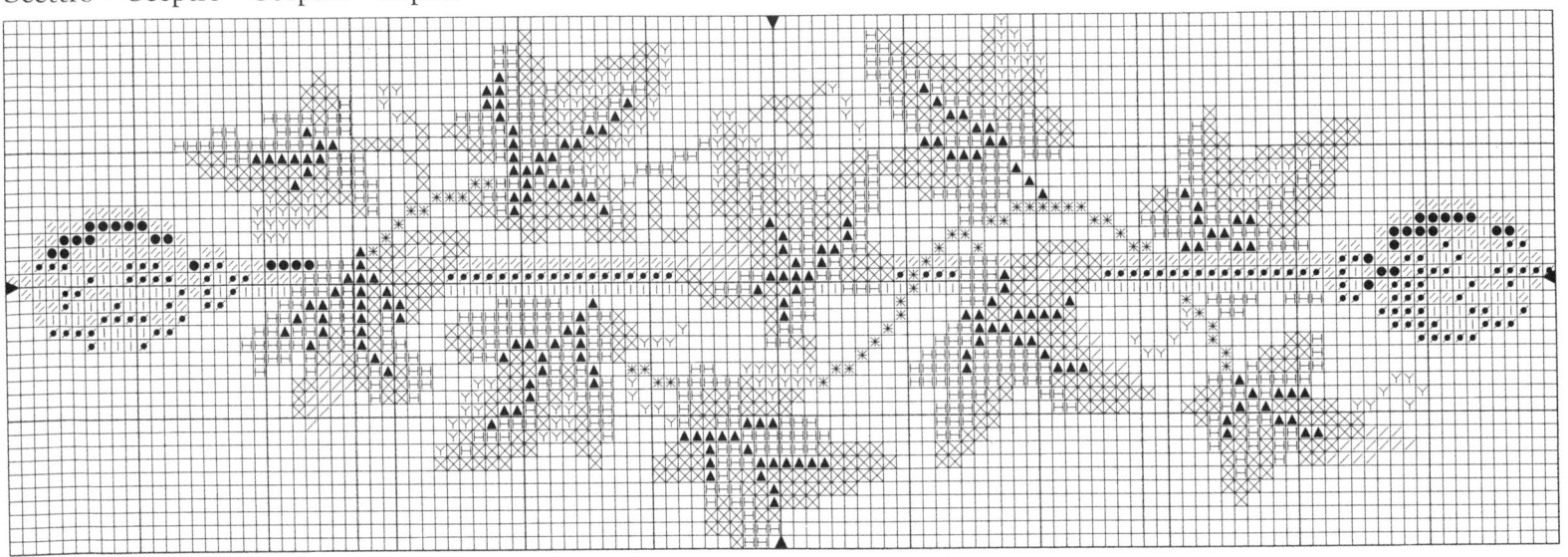

Mouliné

- ¦¦ DMC : 725
- ▲▲ DMC : 500
- HH DMC : 561
- ⊗ DMC : 562
- YY DMC : 563
- ∕∕ DMC : 471
- ✳✳ DMC : 801
- •• DMC : 300
- ∕∕ DMC : 920
- ∕∕ DMC : 976

Cestino con faretra • Panier et carquois • Basket and quiver • Korb mit Köcher

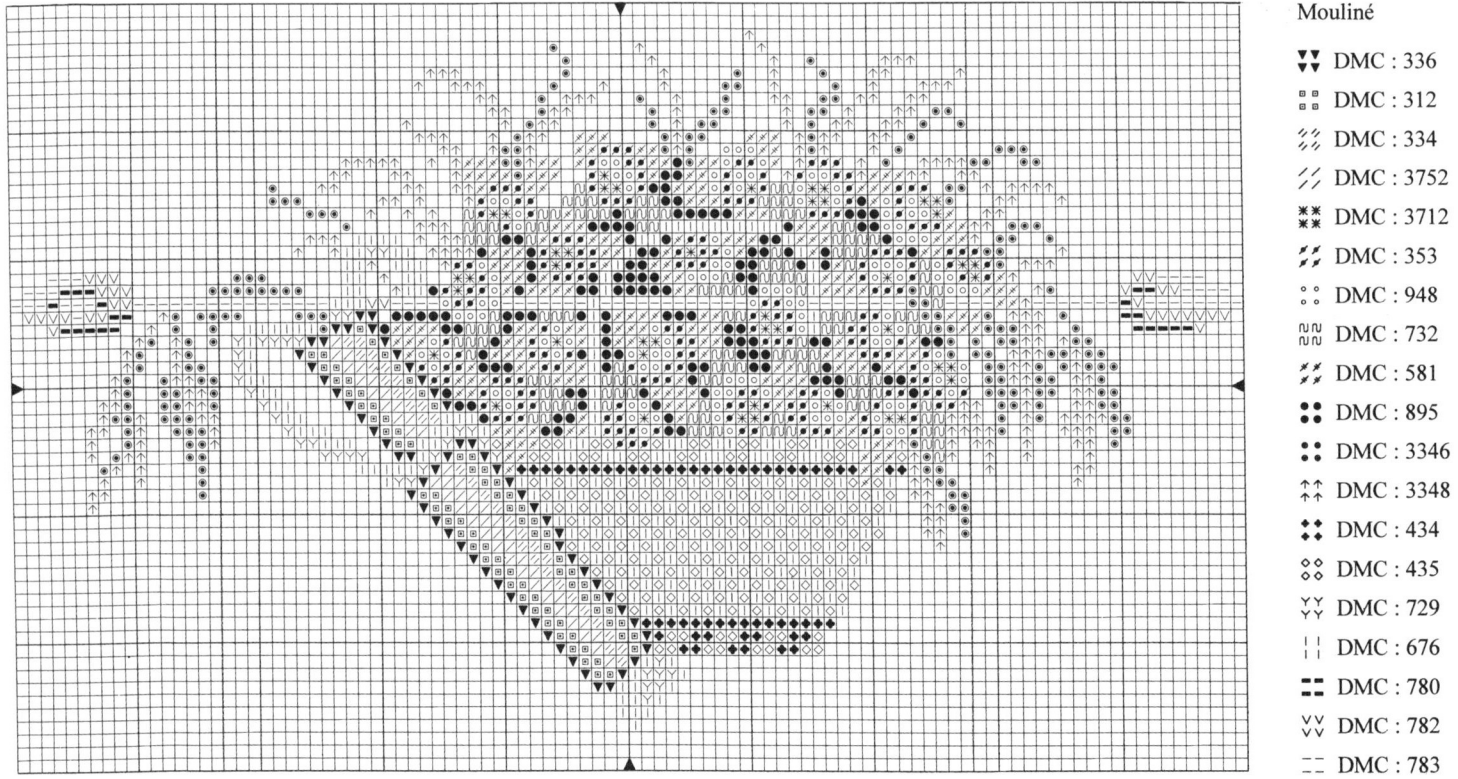

Mouliné

- ▼▼ DMC : 336
- ▫▫ DMC : 312
- ∕∕ DMC : 334
- ∕∕ DMC : 3752
- ✳✳ DMC : 3712
- ∕∕ DMC : 353
- ∘∘ DMC : 948
- ∾∾ DMC : 732
- ∕∕ DMC : 581
- •• DMC : 895
- ∷ DMC : 3346
- ↑↑ DMC : 3348
- ❖❖ DMC : 434
- ○○ DMC : 435
- YY DMC : 729
- ¦¦ DMC : 676
- == DMC : 780
- VV DMC : 782
- -- DMC : 783

• Corbeille de roses et violettes • Basket of roses and violets • Korb mit Rosen und Stiefmütterchen

Mouliné

- DMC : 801
- DMC : 434
- DMC : 680
- DMC : 676
- DMC : 677
- DMC : 823
- DMC : 791
- DMC : 333
- DMC : 340
- DMC : 3747
- DMC : 902
- DMC : 814
- DMC : 3328
- DMC : 760
- DMC : 3779
- DMC : 3774
- DMC : 934
- DMC : 937
- DMC : 470
- DMC : 471
- DMC : 472
- DMC : 829
- DMC : 725

Rametto fiorito • Petite branche fleurie •
Small flowering branch • Blühender Zweig

Mouliné

- DMC : 919
- DMC : 921
- DMC : 402
- DMC : 743
- DMC : 898
- DMC : 829
- DMC : 936
- DMC : 469
- DMC : 471
- DMC : 312
- DMC : 809

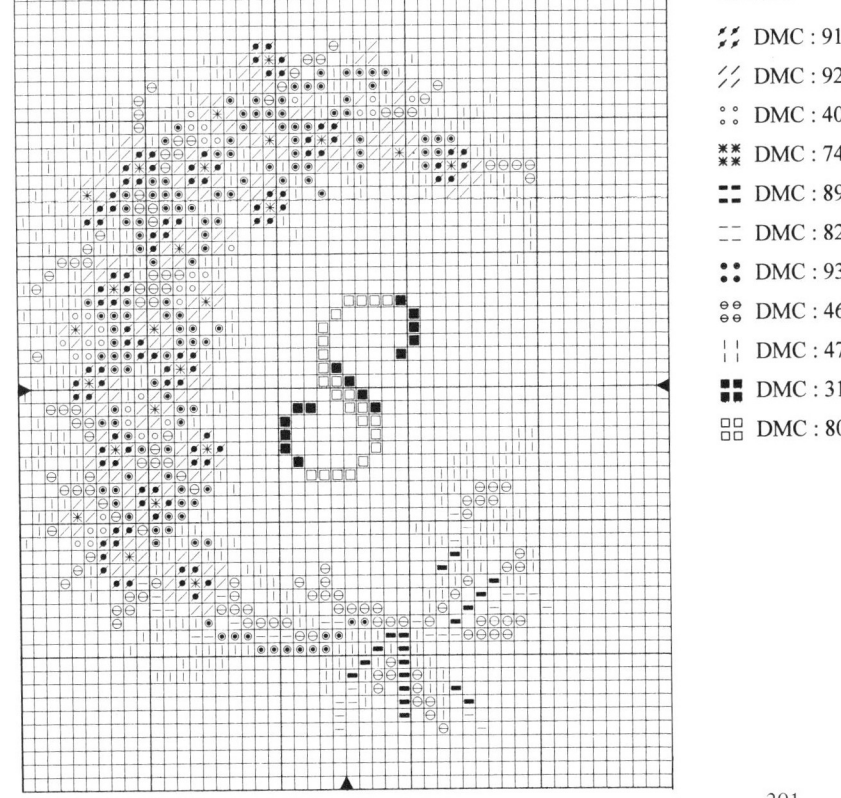

Corno dell'abbondanza • Corne d'abondance • Horn of plenty • Füllhorn

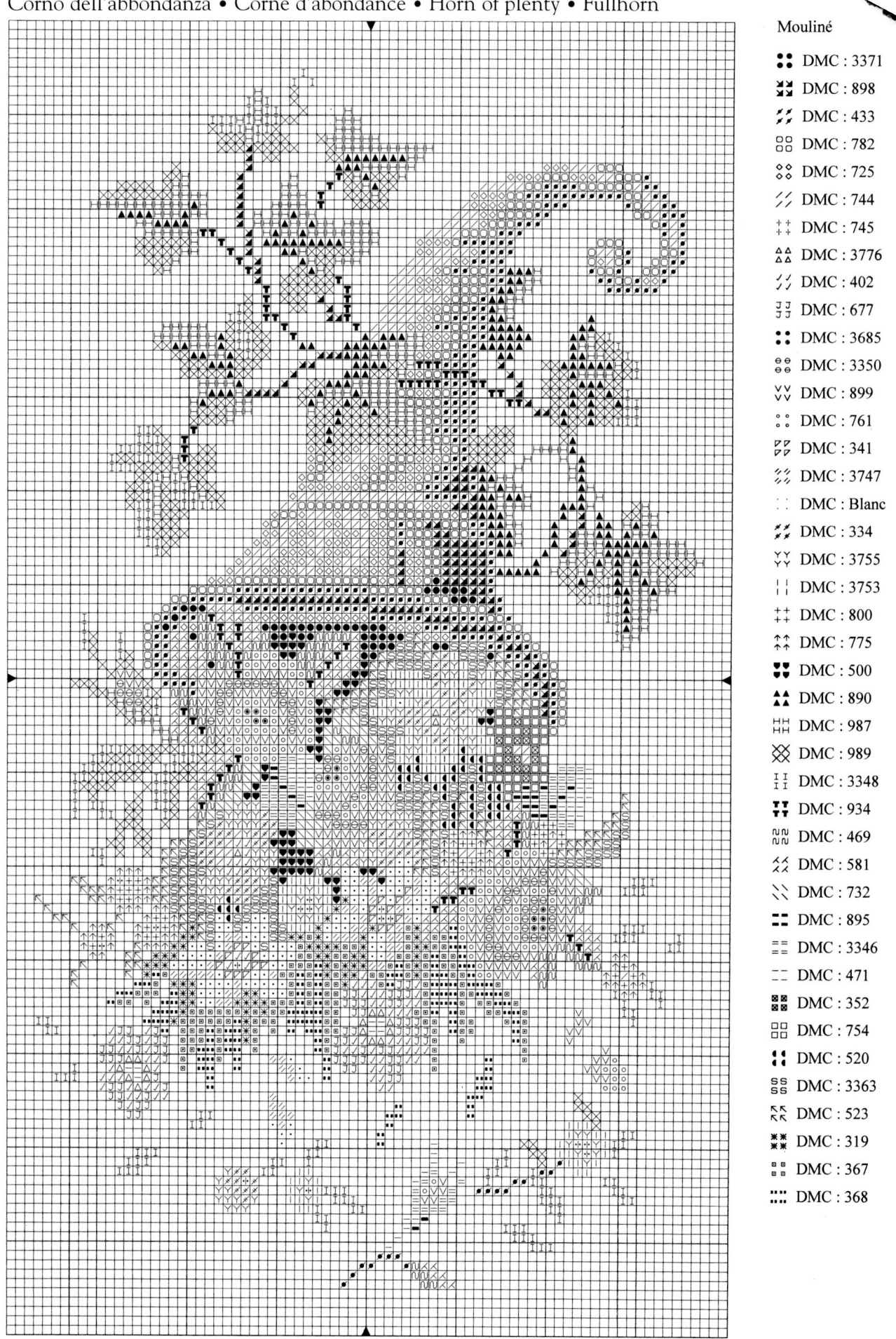

Mouliné

- DMC : 3371
- DMC : 898
- DMC : 433
- DMC : 782
- DMC : 725
- DMC : 744
- DMC : 745
- DMC : 3776
- DMC : 402
- DMC : 677
- DMC : 3685
- DMC : 3350
- DMC : 899
- DMC : 761
- DMC : 341
- DMC : 3747
- DMC : Blanc
- DMC : 334
- DMC : 3755
- DMC : 3753
- DMC : 800
- DMC : 775
- DMC : 500
- DMC : 890
- DMC : 987
- DMC : 989
- DMC : 3348
- DMC : 934
- DMC : 469
- DMC : 581
- DMC : 732
- DMC : 895
- DMC : 3346
- DMC : 471
- DMC : 352
- DMC : 754
- DMC : 520
- DMC : 3363
- DMC : 523
- DMC : 319
- DMC : 367
- DMC : 368

Ramo di rose • Branche de rosier • Rose spray • Rosenzweig

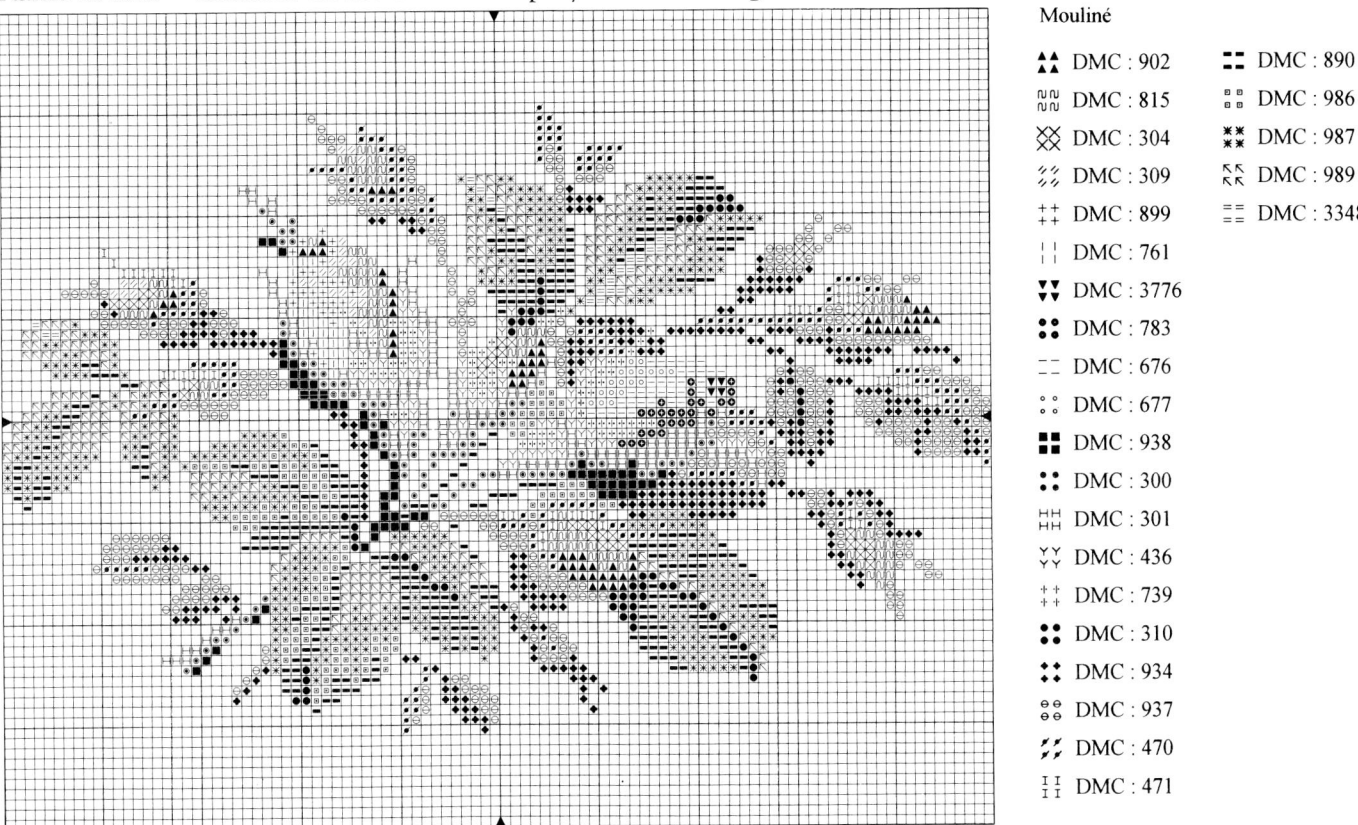

Mouliné

- DMC : 902
- DMC : 815
- DMC : 304
- DMC : 309
- DMC : 899
- DMC : 761
- DMC : 3776
- DMC : 783
- DMC : 676
- DMC : 677
- DMC : 938
- DMC : 300
- DMC : 301
- DMC : 436
- DMC : 739
- DMC : 310
- DMC : 934
- DMC : 937
- DMC : 470
- DMC : 471
- DMC : 890
- DMC : 986
- DMC : 987
- DMC : 989
- DMC : 3348

Boccioli • Fleurs on boutons • Flower buds • Blütenknospen

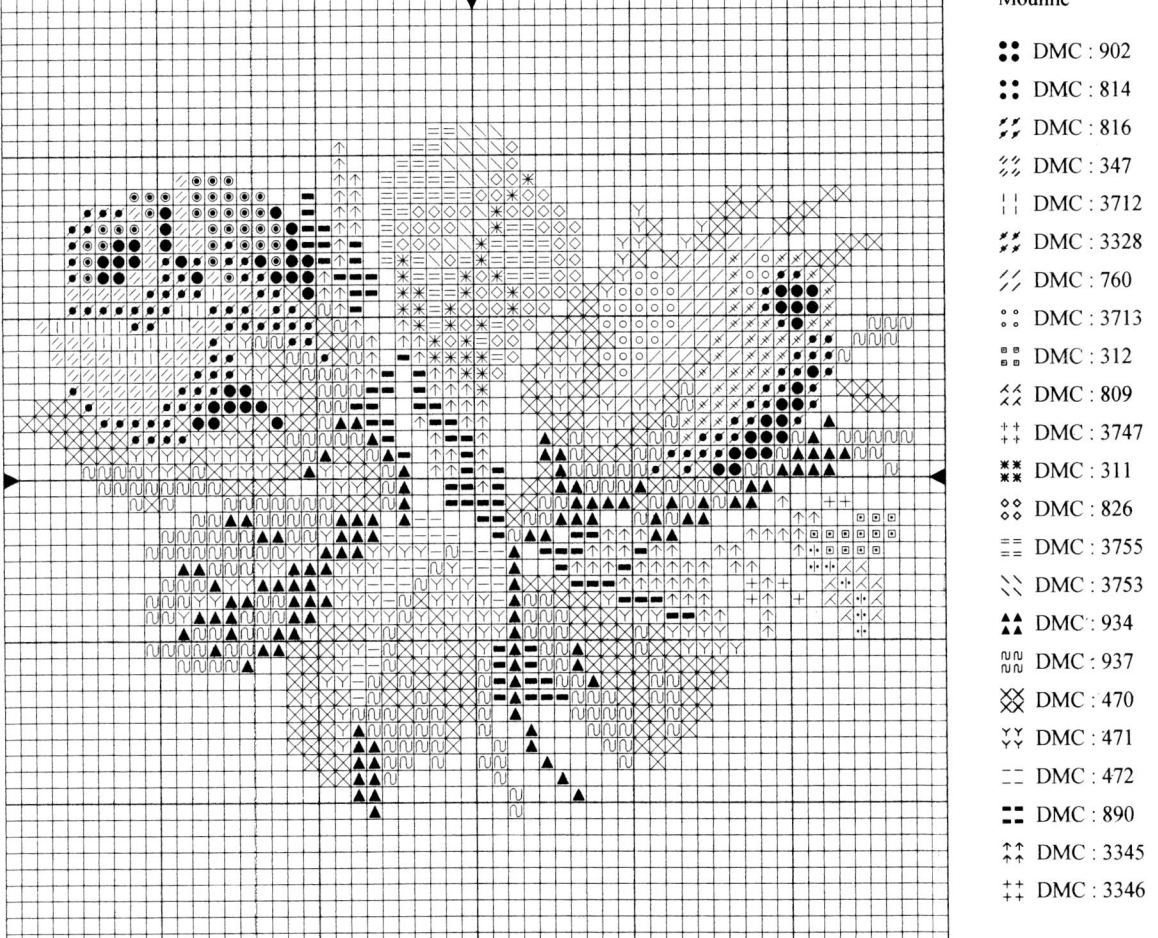

Mouliné

- DMC : 902
- DMC : 814
- DMC : 816
- DMC : 347
- DMC : 3712
- DMC : 3328
- DMC : 760
- DMC : 3713
- DMC : 312
- DMC : 809
- DMC : 3747
- DMC : 311
- DMC : 826
- DMC : 3755
- DMC : 3753
- DMC : 934
- DMC : 937
- DMC : 470
- DMC : 471
- DMC : 472
- DMC : 890
- DMC : 3345
- DMC : 3346

Lira • Lyre • Lyre • Lyra

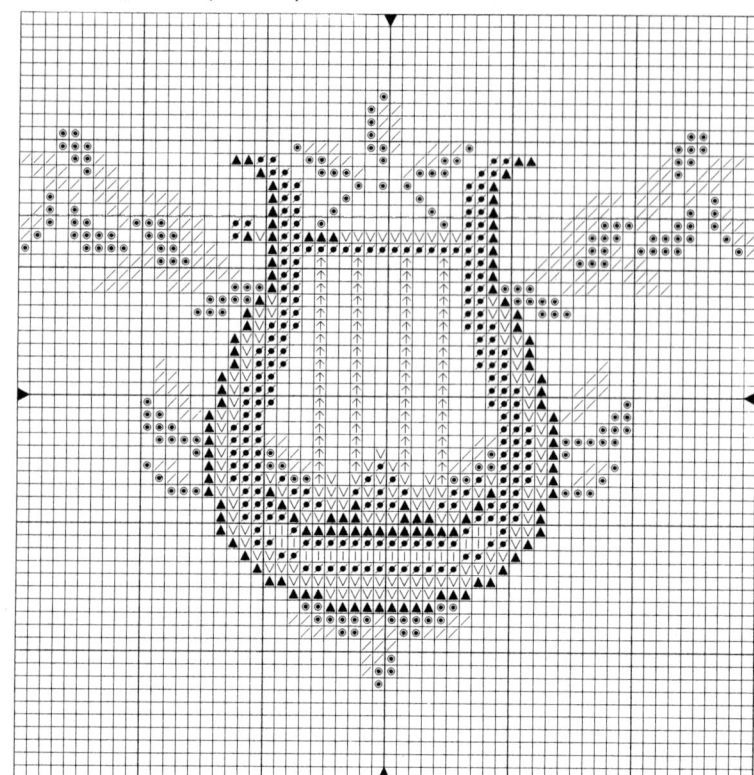

Mouliné

| | DMC : 744
∥ DMC : 725
∨∨ DMC : 782
▲▲ DMC : 434
•• DMC : 937
∥ DMC : 471
↑↑ DMC : 318

Rosone • Rosace • Rosette • Rosette

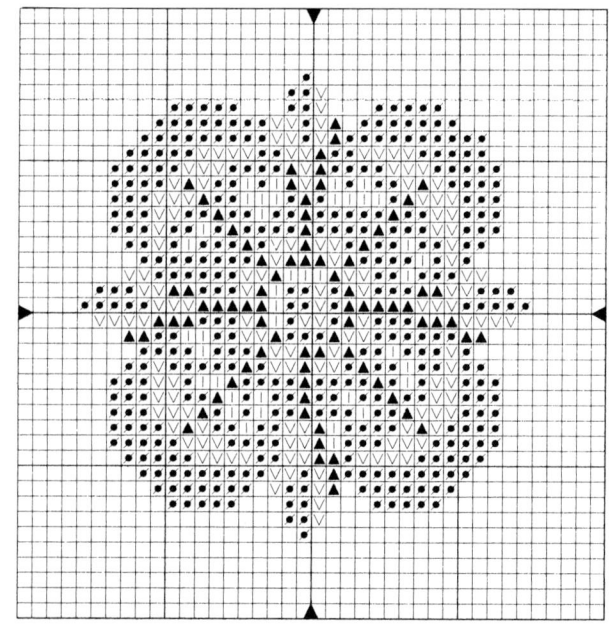

Mouliné

| | DMC : 744
∥ DMC : 725
∨∨ DMC : 782
▲▲ DMC : 780

Faretra • Carquois • Quiver • Köcher

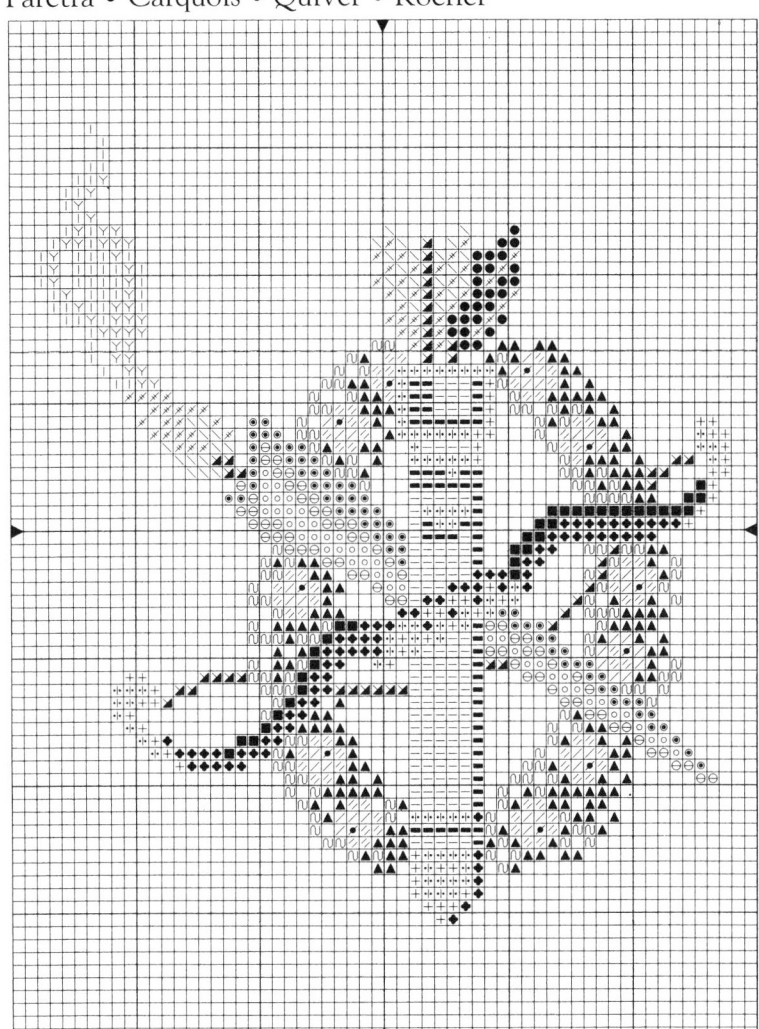

Mouliné

- ▪▪ DMC : 823
- ▫▫ DMC : 791
- ■■ DMC : 938
- ❖❖ DMC : 918
- ✚✚ DMC : 921
- ✚✚ DMC : 783
- ✖✖ DMC : 310
- YY DMC : 318
- || DMC : 3072
- ∴∴ DMC : 3781
- ⊙⊙ DMC : 3032
- ∘∘ DMC : 3033
- ▲▲ DMC : 814
- ⁄⁄ DMC : 816
- \\ DMC : 817
- ▲▲ DMC : 319
- ∽∽ DMC : 3346
- ⁄⁄ DMC : 3685
- ⁄⁄ DMC : 326
- ⁄⁄ DMC : 961

Lance • Lances • Lances • Lanzen

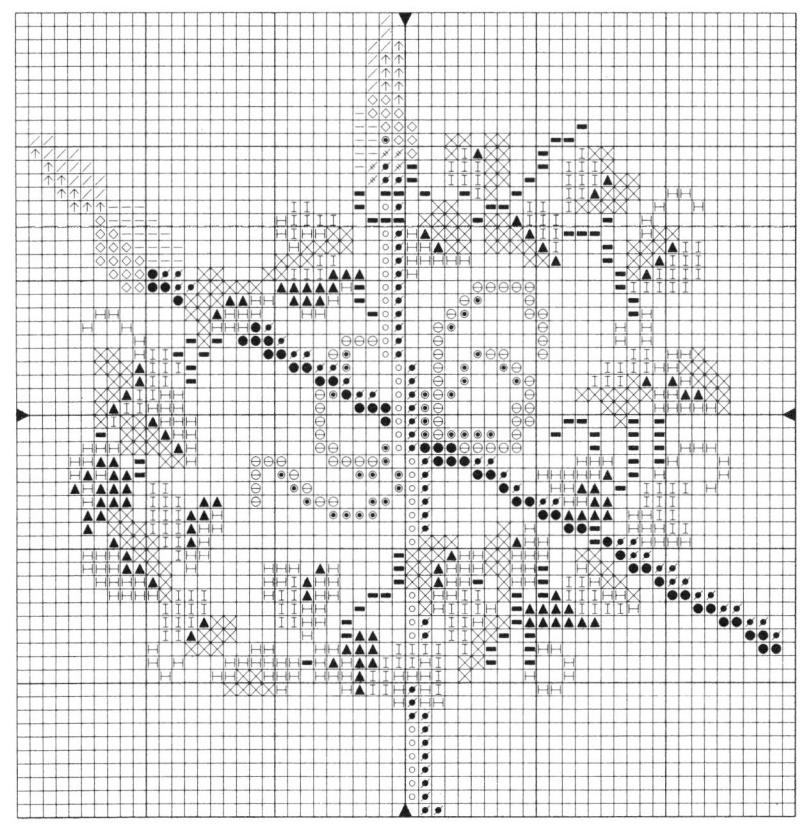

Mouliné

- ▲▲ DMC : 895
- HH DMC : 3346
- ⊠ DMC : 3347
- II DMC : 471
- ▬▬ DMC : 936
- ∷∷ DMC : 938
- ⁄⁄ DMC : 801
- ∘∘ DMC : 433
- ⁄⁄ DMC : 3777
- ◇◇ DMC : 355
- ▬▬ DMC : 356
- ↑↑ DMC : 413
- ⁄⁄ DMC : 414
- ∷∷ DMC : 347
- ⊙⊙ DMC : 3328

Cuore • Coeur • Heart • Herz

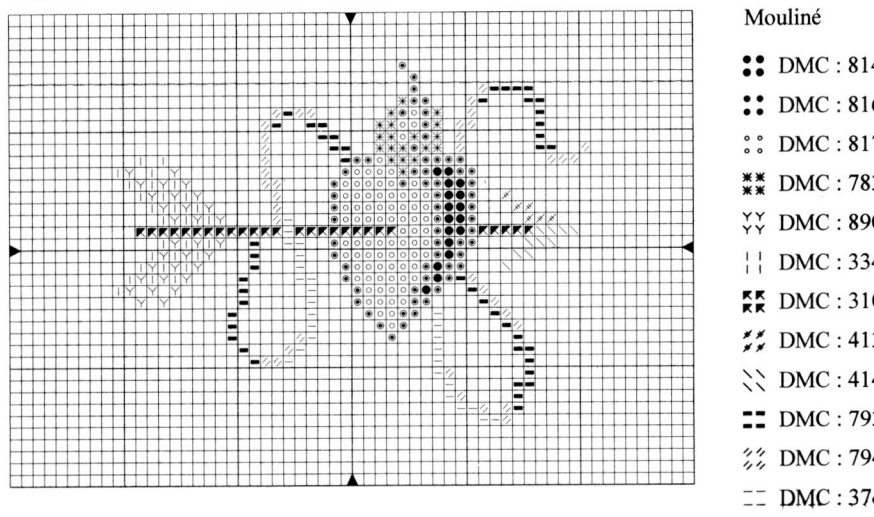

Mouliné

- DMC : 814
- DMC : 816
- DMC : 817
- DMC : 783
- DMC : 890
- DMC : 3345
- DMC : 310
- DMC : 413
- DMC : 414
- DMC : 793
- DMC : 794
- DMC : 3747

Fiaccola • Flambeau • Torch • Fackel

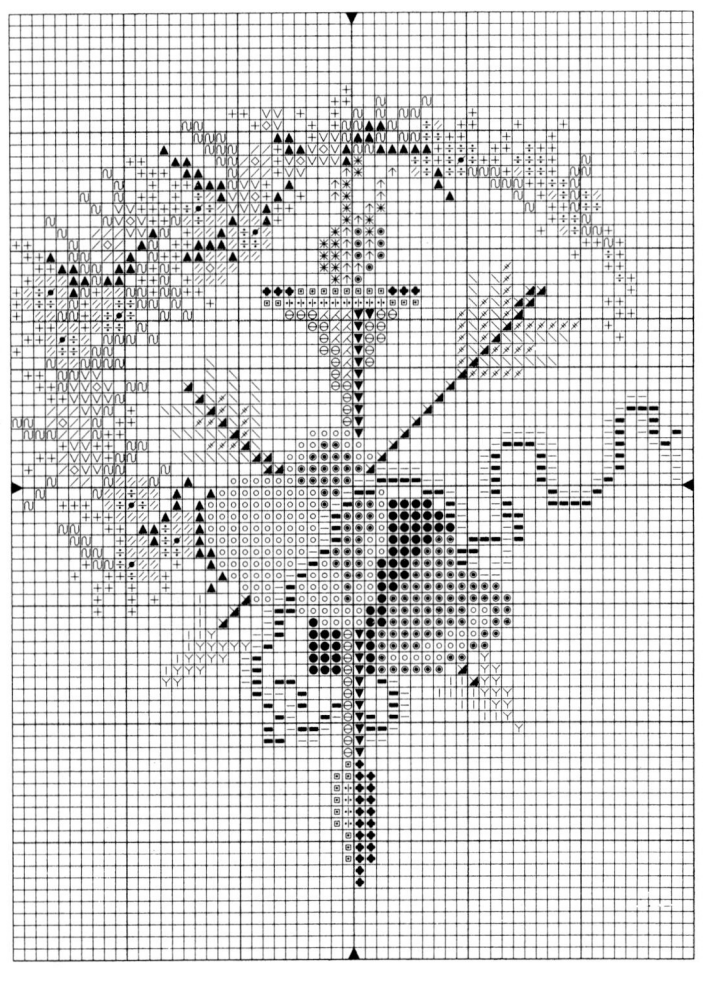

Mouliné

- DMC : 814
- DMC : 816
- DMC : 817
- DMC : 349
- DMC : 900
- DMC : 793
- DMC : 794
- DMC : 3346
- DMC : 3347
- DMC : 3348
- DMC : 326
- DMC : 961
- DMC : 3716
- DMC : 792
- DMC : 3807
- DMC : 676
- DMC : 310
- DMC : 317
- DMC : 318
- DMC : 315
- DMC : 3721
- DMC : 823
- DMC : 791
- DMC : 793
- DMC : 918
- DMC : 921
- DMC : 783

Bibliography

M. Carmignani, preface to *A piccoli punti* (Milan: De Agostini, 1991, 1995).

A. Christie, *Autobiography* (London: Collins 1977).

L. Goldoni, *Maria Luigia, donna in carriera* (Milan: Rizzoli, 1993).

E. H. Gombrich, *Il senso dell'ordine. Studio sulla psicologia dell'arte decorativa* (Turin: Einaudi, 1984).

G. Himmelheber, *Biedermeier 1805-1815* (Munich: Prestel, 1989).

W. M. Johnston, *Vienna, Vienna...* (Milan: A. Mondadori, 1981).

J. Landwehr-Vogels, *Historische kruissteekpatronen* (Eden: Zomer & Keuning Bocken B. V., 1984).

M. Praz, *La filosofia dell'arredamento* (Milan: Longanesi, 1964).

M. G. Proctor, *Victorian Canvas Work. Berlin Wool Work* (London: B. T. Batsford Limited, 1972).

I. Schiel, *Maria Luigia* (Milan: Longanesi, 1983).

R. Serena, *A piccoli punti* (Milan: De Agostini, 1991, 1995).

A. Wilkie, *Biedermeier* (Milan: A. Mondadori, 1987).

Maria Luigia donna e sovrana. Una corte europea a Parma 1815-1847, catalogue (Parma: Ugo Guanda, 1992).

Vienne 1815-1848 à l'époque Biedermeier, catalogue (Paris: P. Gentil, 1990).

Printed in Italy, August 1998